GETTING KIDS TO MIX

GETTING KIDS
TO MIX

LEN WOODS

VICTOR BOOKS
A DIVISION OF SCRIPTURE PRESS PUBLICATIONS INC.
USA CANADA ENGLAND

Cover Design: Joe DeLeon
Illustrations: Arnie Ten
ISBN 1-56476-115-0

Produced for Victor Books by the Livingstone Corporation.
David R. Veerman, Daryl J. Lucas, Kathleen Ristow, and
Brenda James Todd, project staff.

1 2 3 4 5 6 7 8 9 10 Printing/Year 97 96 95 94 93
Printed in the United States of America

This book is dedicated with love
to the two incredible people
with whom I have the privilege
of "mixing and mingling"
on a daily basis—
my wife Cindi
and my son Walter.

Acknowledgements

Special thanks to Christ Community Church
and The Fellowship at Louisiana Tech
for being the "guinea pigs" of this project.
I can't think of two groups in the whole world
with whom I'd rather be involved.
I am also indebted to my creative friends
at The Livingstone Corporation.

Contents

Foreword

• This book will change your life!

• One of the year's 10 best!

• I give it four stars!

• A guaranteed best-seller, Gold Medallion winner, and shoo-in for the Pulitzer Prize!

• This book made me what I am today!

• I can hardly wait for the movie!

As I was thinking of what I could write as a foreword for a book of mixers, I struggled with the right phrase, the clever gambit, the exciting attention-getting opener. I came up blank. So instead of using any exaggerated claims or phony ploys (like those above, which undoubtedly caught your eye), I decided to be honest. So here goes. See what you think.

"What do you do at those meetings anyway, just play games?" The concerned father pointed his finger at me as he questioned the validity of my ministry in his own subtle way. All he had heard from his daughter about the youth group was that it was fun . . . and in his mind, that spelled trouble. For the next few minutes I tried to explain how crowdbreakers and other games were helpful educational tools—I'm not sure he was convinced.

Unfortunately some folks still believe that ministry has to be serious to be meaningful. Fun is OK, but it's important to get down to the deeper, spiritual issues.

During more than three decades of youth ministry, I have found that laughter and true spirituality are not contradictory or mutually exclusive. In fact, sometimes the ministry can be quite enjoyable and, at times, downright hilarious. Games, skits, openers, starters, mixers—all are invaluable tools for helping to build relationships, begin discussion, break-down barriers, and reinforce biblical truth.

Perhaps the most useful game is the "mixer," an event designed to get group members mingling and meeting, breaking down social barriers and helping people open up to each other and to the truth. Good mixers get people talking with each other, laughing together, and learning from each other.

Len Woods is the master of the mixer (re: mixmaster). He creates, writes, and uses them in his work. I met Len several years ago when I was the Director of Southeast Louisiana Campus Life and he was the Minister of Youth at the Chapel On the Campus in Baton Rouge. I thought he was crazy . . . but he had a terrific ministry in that community. Len Woods is still crazy, and he is still having a terrific ministry, now with students in Ruston, Louisiana.

Len Woods is also one of the most creative people I have ever met, twisting, tweaking, and turning rough ideas into effective games, activities, programs, and lessons. And he loves to have a good time—humor permeates all his work.

In this book, we have the opportunity to catch a slice of Len's ministry. Mr. "Mix-master" has written a book full of mixers for us to use with groups of all sizes. Not only has he written these games, he's also used them—they're good—they work. Len has packed 101 of these puppies in here, along with some other goodies. Most of the mixers use a sheet to be distributed to group members—those sheets are included, ready to be copied and used. In fact, all you have to do is think through your group and the meeting, choose the appropriate mixer, add people, and stir.

The mixers in this book are guaranteed to be fun, useful, effective . . . and a little crazy. Happy mixing!

Dave Veerman

Introduction

Is there anything more fulfilling than seeing God change a life?

If there is I don't know what that thing would be.

But after more than thirteen years of ministry to teenagers, collegiates, and adults, I am more convinced than ever that lifechange and spiritual maturity *cannot* happen in isolation. That's because God designed us to function in relationships with others. It's only as we join with other believers in living out the "one another" commands of the New Testament that we are changed and the world is impacted.

Ah, but there's the rub. How can I love someone I hardly know? How likely are you to bear the burdens of another, when you have no idea what those burdens are?

That's the premise behind this simple book.

There is no deep theology, no sociological theory here. Just one hundred and one exercises that I've used to break down barriers and build bridges in the groups I've had the privilege of leading.

Do you have a group of total strangers? Inside you'll find mixers to help your group members learn each others' names. Is your group too stiff and tense? Loosen them up with a crazy crowdbreaker. Do your group members know each others' likes and dislikes? A get-acquainted exercise can move them to a new level of understanding and appreciation. Do your group conversations tend to be predictable and superficial . . . and dull? Liven things up with a thought-provoking discussion starter. Is your group healthy and growing? Challenge your members to risk going even deeper with a self-revelation game.

I truly believe this book can play a small role in helping your group become more honest, more understanding, and more fun. If so, it will have been worth it.

And if not, well, at least I earned enough in advance fees to help pay for a badly-needed root canal.

Part One:

MEETING & GREETING

The Alphabet Name Game

Instructions to Leaders:

■ This game helps large or small groups learn each others' names.
■ Give each person a copy of the sheet below.
■ Play until someone wins (this is unlikely, unless Malcolm X and Dweezil Zappa are in your group) or for 5–7 minutes.

COVER THE INSTRUCTIONS ABOVE THIS LINE BEFORE PHOTOCOPYING THIS HANDOUT FOR YOUR GROUP.

- -

The Alphabet Name Game

You have five minutes to meet as many people as possible and find names—first, middle, or last—for each letter of the alphabet. Only one letter per person is allowed!

A	N
B	O
C	P
D	Q
E	R
F	S
G	T
H	U
I	V
J	W
K	X
L	Y
M	Z

Name Tag Shuffle

Instructions to Leaders:

■ This game helps small- to medium-sized groups (12–50 people) learn each others' names.
■ This mixer takes only 5–7 minutes.

Here's how it works:

1. Fill out a name tag for every person in the room. (This is best done as people are arriving for the meeting.)
2. When the meeting begins, mix up the name tags and distribute them face down—one per person.
3. Have each person stick that name tag on the back of someone else *without that person seeing the name.*
4. When you give the signal, each individual will mill about the room asking questions to try to determine the name on his or her back.
5. All questions must be "yes" or "no" type questions. (For example, "Is the person on my back a male?" "Does that person have blonde hair?" etc.)
6. Continue for a set period of time (five to seven minutes) or until everyone has guessed the name on his or her back.

*Name Ping-Pong**

Instructions to Leaders:

■ This mixer helps small- to medium-sized groups (12–50) learn each others' names.
■ It can be completed in about 10 minutes.

Here's how it works:

1. Have your group sit in a circle. (If you have a group of more than 20, have two circles playing at once.)
2. Give each person a hymnbook or some other similar hard-cover book.
3. The object of the game is to use the books to bat a Ping-Pong ball back and forth across (and around) the circle, and for the entire group to chant in unison the name of each person hitting the ball as he or she hits it.
4. A foam ball can be substituted (and may be preferred since it can be batted with barehands).

*This mixer was created by Bret Hinkie, Minister to Youth at Christ Community Church in Ruston, LA.

Name Association

Instructions to Leaders:

■ This game helps small- to medium-sized groups learn each others' names.
■ This mixer takes only 5–7 minutes.

Here's how it works:

1. This is a very old name-learning game in which players sit in a big circle. Your circle(s) should contain no more than 25–30 people. Subdivide your group (if necessary) accordingly.
2. The game can be played many ways, but typically it involves player number one saying his or her name and a favorite hobby or food or ice cream flavor (pick a category). (Examples: "My name is Kimberly and I like to hike"; or "My name is Sharon and I like Mexican food"; or "My name is Wade and I like strawberry ice cream.")
3. The second player repeats what the previous player said and adds his or her own name and favorite item. The third player then restates the names and favorites of the first two players and then adds his or her own information!
4. Continue until you have gone all the way around the circle.
5. This game requires a great deal of concentration, but it is an excellent way to help new groups learn each others' names.

Initial Soup

Instructions to Leaders:

■ This mixer is a great exercise for learning names and takes only 7–10 minutes.
■ You will need to provide something to write with and something to write on for each small group that participates.

Here's how it works:

1. Divide your group members into small groups of 5–7 people each.
2. Give each group a big piece of poster board/butcher paper/newsprint.
3. Have each group member share his or her full name.
4. Write down all the initials from your group across the top of the page. (Example: A group composed of Adina Faye Jones, John Richard Love, Thomas Benton Hilton, Alyson Patrice Dalton, Ivan Arabie III, and Sue Ellen Woods would get the initials A, F, J, J, R, L, T, B, H, A, P, D, I, A, S, E, and W.
5. Give each group five minutes to think of all the words they can (three letters or more) using their combined initials.
6. No word can use the same letter more than once—unless, of course, two or more people have the same initial. (Example: The group above would get credit for "shaped" and "father" and "data" but not for "seed," as there is only one "e.")
7. Teams get points as follows:
   1 point for every three-letter word.
   2 points for each four-letter word.
   3 points for five-letter words.
   5 points for six-letter words.
   8 points for seven-letter words.
   10 points for eight-letter (or more) words.
8. So that each team has *at least* three vowels among their initials, they may "trade in" one, two, or three of their consonant initials for any of the "second letter" vowels found in their names. [Example: Samantha Hill, John Jay Hodges, Jennifer Roberts, and Cindi Lee Witmer could trade in up to three of their initials (S, H, J, J, H, J, R, C, L, and W), which are all consonants. The vowels they could choose from would be Samantha Hill, John Jay Hodges, Jennifer Roberts, and Cindi Lee Witmer. This team would probably be wise to trade in two of their J's and one of their H's for maybe an A, an I, and an E.]
9. Tally up the scores and proclaim a winner.

Crazy Dots

Instructions to Leaders:

- ■ This game helps medium- to large-size groups get acquainted.
- ■ For best results, you will want to divide into smaller, more manageable groups of 6–10 (for example, if you have 24 participants, break down into three groups of 8).
- ■ Since this is a competition, you will need at least two teams of six persons each.
- ■ Divide your group using different colored dots. You can use either store-bought dots (i.e., round stickers used as garage sale price tags—available at discount stores like Wal-Mart or K-mart in a number of colors), or you can use different colored marker pens and draw your own ink dots on cheeks, foreheads, hands, or name tags.
- ■ Give each person a copy of the handout below.

COVER THE INSTRUCTIONS ABOVE THIS LINE BEFORE PHOTOCOPYING THIS HANDOUT FOR YOUR GROUP.

- -

Crazy Dots

Instructions to Participants:

1. Find all the members of your group (all the people in the room who have the same color dot).
2. As a team, work your way through the following instructions as quickly and as accurately as possible.
3. Elect a team captain.
4. Sit down in a circle and have each person one at a time say his or her name and "what I want to be when I grow up."
5. Stand up, divide your team into two groups and loudly sing *Row, Row, Row Your Boat* **three times in rounds!**
6. Build a six-person pyramid, while chanting, "Go! Go! Go! . . . "
7. One letter at a time, spell out the first name of your team leader by having two or three team members at a time lie on the floor in the shape of that letter. As each letter is completed, the entire team must yell out the name of that letter.
8. Pick up your captain on your shoulders and parade him or her around the room, taunting the other teams and chanting, "We're number one!" After one lap around the room, put your captain down, cheer wildly, and go back to your group's original spot.

Crazy Dots 2

Instructions to Leaders:

- This mixer works exactly like Crazy Dots.
- This game is ideal for helping medium- to large-size groups get acquainted.
- For best results, you will want to divide into smaller, more manageable groups of 6–10 (for example, if you have 24 participants, break down into three groups of 8).
- Since this is a competition, you will need at least two teams of six persons each.
- Divide your group using different colored dots. You can use either store-bought dots (i.e., round stickers used as garage sale price tags—available at discount stores like Wal-Mart or Kmart in a number of colors), or you can use different colored marker pens and draw dots on cheeks, foreheads, or hands.
- If you are not familiar with "The Blue Danube," pick another well-known classical song that you can demonstrate for your group (see instruction seven below).
- Give each person a copy of the handout below.

COVER THE INSTRUCTIONS ABOVE THIS LINE BEFORE PHOTOCOPYING THIS HANDOUT FOR YOUR GROUP.

- -

Crazy Dots 2

Instructions to Participants:

1. Find all the members of your group (all the people in the room who have the same color dot).
2. As a team, work your way through the following instructions as quickly and as accurately as possible.
3. Elect a team captain.
4. Sit down in a circle and have each person one at a time say his or her name and describe "my dream house."
5. Still sitting on the floor, get in a tight circle, back-to-back. With arms locked together, and solely by pushing against each others' backs, *try to stand up all together.*
6. Have your group form a circle—facing inward—and *sing two verses of "The Hokey Pokey"* (the two verses about "putting your right and left legs in and shaking them all about" will suffice!)
7. Get at least two couples (preferably male-female combinations) to pair up and *waltz together* for 10 seconds while the rest of the group hums "The Blue Danube."
8. Pretend to be wild geese flying south for the winter. In V-formation, with your team captain leading the way, your entire team should *flap and honk* its way around the room. When you have completed your "goose lap," shake hands with your teammates and go back to your original spot.

People Pandemonium

Instructions to Leaders:

■ This mixer/crowdbreaker combines crazy activity and opportunities for getting acquainted.
■ This mixer/crowdbreaker works best in groups of 20 and up.
■ You can play this as a competition and give out a prize, or you can set a time limit.
■ Give each person a copy of the handout below.

COVER THE INSTRUCTIONS ABOVE THIS LINE BEFORE PHOTOCOPYING THIS HANDOUT FOR YOUR GROUP.

- -

People Pandemonium

As quickly and accurately as possible, work your way through the following list.

1. Go up to someone of the opposite sex, pretend you're a skunk, and then pretend to spray that person with a bad aroma (like real skunks do).
  He or she should sign here:
2. Grab a partner, exchange names, shake hands, then drop down and do 15 sit-ups or push-ups together. Sign each other's sheet here:
3. Try to break dance or moon-walk and get a witness to initial here:
4. Find someone who has (or has had) braces, get them to say "cheese." You pretend to take his or her picture. He or she should sign here:
5. Stop someone with your same eye color and sing these lyrics together (to the tune of "Happy Birthday to You"):
    I'm so glad to meet you,
    In the midst of this zoo!
    Please initial my paper—
    I'll do the same thing for you.
  Get your partner's initials here:

6. Stand on a chair and give a 15 second speech on "How My School Could Be Improved." Get a witness to sign here:
7. Get the initials of someone who can tell you the two middle names of former President George Bush:
8. Find a partner and pretend to ride a bicycle built for two around the room—backwards. Your partner signs here:
9. Get with three other people and the four of you put your arms around the necks of each other (like girls in a chorus line) and then march across the room bumping into people while chanting, "We won't stop! We won't stop! We won't stop for a lollipop!" Get two of your teammates to initial here:
10. Find someone who is smiling or laughing and get him or her to sign here:

Beach-O-Rama

Instructions to Leaders:

■ This mixer/crowdbreaker combines crazy activity and opportunities for getting acquainted.
■ This mixer/crowdbreaker works best in groups of 20 and up.
■ This mixer/crowdbreaker is great during the summer or during trips to beach areas.
■ Play this as a competition and give out a prize, or simply set a time limit.
■ Give each person a copy of the handout below.

- -

Beach-O-Rama

As quickly and accurately as possible, work your way through the following list.

1. Find a fair-skinned person and ask, "Wow! How'd you get such a great tan?" He or she should sign here:
2. Get with three other people. Two of you circle the other two, humming the theme song from the movie *Jaws,* while the other two scream for 10 seconds. One person initials here:
3. Walk around the room with your hands out (like you're surfing) and say to five different people, "I can outsurf you and your whole family any day of the week!"
   The fifth person signs here:
4. Ask three different people to be your "Beach Baby." The third signs here:
5. Go up to someone you barely know and give him or her a 10 second speech on why the ocean tastes salty. He or she initials here:
6. Jump up and down 10 times, waving your arms and then yell, "Everybody out of the water!" Get a witness to sign here:
7. Tell someone this riddle and then fall on the floor and laugh hysterically for five full seconds:

   Q: Do you know why you can never get hungry at the beach?
   A: Because of the sand which is (sandwiches) there!

   That person initials here:

8. Ask someone what the weather forecast is for tomorrow and then giggle uncontrollably. He or she should sign here:
9. Get with two other people, lie on the floor, and pretend to swim, while singing:
   "This is the way we swim to Hawaii, swim to Hawaii, swim to Hawaii. This is the way we swim to Hawaii, so early in the morning." Get one of your partners to initial here:

Winter Wackiness

Instructions to Leaders:

■ This mixer/crowdbreaker combines crazy activity and opportunities for getting acquainted.

■ This mixer/crowdbreaker works best in groups of 20 and up.

■ This mixer/crowdbreaker is great during winter ski trips or in hilly retreat settings, or during the holidays.

■ Give each person a copy of the handout below.

■ Play as a competition and give out a prize, or simply set a time limit.

COVER THE INSTRUCTIONS ABOVE THIS LINE BEFORE PHOTOCOPYING THIS HANDOUT FOR YOUR GROUP.

- -

Winter Wackiness

As quickly and accurately as possible, work your way through the following list.

1. Sit in a chair by someone you know well or fairly well. Pretend that person is a complete stranger and you are on a ski lift together. Act out what you would do and say. He or she signs here:

2. Get with three other people. Imitate champion ice skaters and slide your way around the room twice. Get one of your partners to initial here:

3. Grab someone and together sing two lines of any song you can think of that has the word "snow" in it. Get that person to put his or her John Hancock right here:

4. Sit down with two others and share your favorite winter activity. One of them signs here:

5. Join hands with someone else and run around the room for 10 seconds as though you were catching snowflakes on your tongues. Your partner initials here:

6. Jump up on a chair, look out the window, get a frightened look on your face, and shout "Avalanche!" Get a witness to sign here:

7. Wish five people "Season's Greetings!" The fifth initials here:

8. Pull someone aside and together pretend to be suffering from hypothermia. Shivering, shaking, and with chattering teeth, find someone older and whine, "It's cold in here! Turn on the heat!" That person signs here:

9. Find three other people and together pretend to bobsled your way around the room. One of them signs here:

10. Do your best fake sneeze. Have the person who initialed number 5 above rate you here on a scale of 1–10 (1 is "fake beyond words"; 10 is "so real I thought I had snot on me"):

Tiger-Tarzan-Jane

Instructions to Leaders:

- This game is a take-off on the old children's game "Paper, Rock & Scissors."
- This game is active, lots of fun, and gives people a chance to pair off and meet several new folks.
- This game can be played as an elimination event until you have a single "Tiger-Tarzan-Jane" champion.
- This competition can be completed in a relatively short time (10 minutes or less)
- This game requires no materials or advance preparation.

Here's how to explain this game to your group:

1. Ask them if they have ever played "Paper, Rock & Scissors" (Most will say "yes.")
2. Tell them *this* game ("Tiger-Tarzan-Jane") is similar (only the motions are different).
3. Explain the various actions in the game:
    - The symbol for "Tiger" is a growling sound together with upraised arms, like a big cat pouncing on its prey.
    - The symbol for "Tarzan" is the famous "ah-ah-ah" Tarzan yell together with a muscle-man pose (biceps bulging).
    - The symbol for "Jane" is a sexy "Hi there" greeting with hands on hips.

4. Explain the rules:
    - Players are to pair up, exchange names, shake hands, and stand back to back.
    - On the count of three, they will spin around, making one of the three noises just mentioned, together with the appropriate pose.
    - The winner of each pairing is determined by the following rules:
        (a) Tarzan always conquers the tiger.
        (b) The tiger always conquers Jane.
        (c) Jane always conquers Tarzan (feel free to use this rule as a great teaching moment!).
    - After each round, pair up the winners and continue eliminating players until you are down to just two finalists.
    - In the final championship round, play best two out of three.
    - Up until the finals, when competitors *draw* (i.e., strike the same pose), they remain in the competition paired up against the same person. But if the players draw a second time, both are out of the competition.

Barnyard at Night

Instructions to Leaders:

■ This game is active, lots of fun, and gives people a chance to meet others.
■ This game works best with medium-sized groups (25–40 individuals).
■ This mixer can also be used as a way of breaking up into small groups for other exercises.
■ Make sure you remove any objects from the room that might *get* damaged or *cause* damage by or to people stumbling around in the dark.

Here's how it works:

1. Give each person a slip a paper with the name of a barnyard animal on it. (There should be at least two of each animal and larger groups may assign as many as six or eight players per animal.)
2. Tell participants that they are not to reveal what animal they are until you give the signal.
3. State that the object of this game is for each person to hook up with all the other "like animals" in the room as quickly as possible. (For example, cows with cows, sheep with sheep, etc.)
4. Explain that the game will begin when you turn out the lights. At that time each person should begin making his or her animal sound, and move about the dark room, until he or she has found everyone else who is making that same sound. Sounds are as follows:

   ■ Horse–neigh   ■ Cow–moo   ■ Dog–bark
   ■ Sheep–bleat   ■ Duck–quack   ■ Cat–meow
   ■ Frog–croak   ■ Pig–oink   ■ Pigeon–coo
   ■ Chicken–cluck   ■ Rooster–crow ■ Goose–honk

5. After a few minutes turn on the lights and see who is still searching.
6. In their "animal groups," have people exchange names and one or two other facts about themselves (for example, preferred brand of toothpaste, plans after graduation, favorite barnyard animal, family history, etc.).

Alphafeet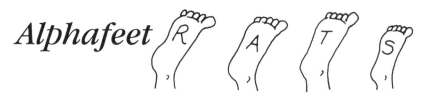

Instructions to Leaders:

■ This game is active, lots of fun, and gives folks a chance to meet someone new.
■ This game is excellent with small- to medium-sized groups (8–40 individuals).
■ Make sure you have a fairly large area in which to play this game. (Players will be lying on the floor and rolling over each other.)

Here's how it works:

1. Break them into groups of four.
2. Have each team pick a captain (someone who can print nicely). (You may wish at this point to give the teams two or three get acquainted questions to discuss before jumping into the competition. See appendix 2.)
3. Have the other three members of each team remove their shoes and socks.
4. Give each captain a felt-tip marker. (Test it first and make sure it writes clearly and legibly on human skin!)
5. Have the captains of each team write the following letters on the bottoms of their team members' feet (one letter per foot): A, E, L, R, S, T
6. Explain that the various teams will now race each other in spelling out words which you, the leader, will call out.
7. All contestants must be standing when you say the word to be spelled out.
8. When you say go, players may fall to the floor and get their "lettered feet" in the right order.
9. The team captain is to coach and make sure his or her team spells the word correctly.

Words for Teams to Spell:

eat, stale, rates, sat, least, rats, slat, salt, tea

Note: Writing the letters on someone's bare feet is literally a ticklish situation! Most people laugh and wiggle uncontrollably. However, if your group would balk at the idea of "exposing their floormost flesh," you might want to consider writing the letters on index cards and taping these to the bottom of the players' shoes.

Raise Your Hand

Instructions to Leaders:

■ This game is excellent for medium- to large-sized groups (40–100+ people).
■ While this game doesn't call for any one-on-one interaction, it does allow folks to identify others in the room with similar (and/or unusual) interests and experiences and may pave the way for later conversation.
■ This game requires no advance preparation.

Here's how it works:

Instruct people to raise their hands when any of the following statements are true of them.

Raise Your Hand . . .

1. If you have been snow skiing.
2. If you are one of four or more children.
3. If you have completed a 10K run.
4. If you have shaken hands with a U.S. President.
5. If you are fluent in a foreign language.
6. If you can touch your tongue to your nose.
7. If you are related to someone famous.
8. If you have fainted in public.
9. If you have won a contest of any kind.
10. If you have more than two pets in your home.
11. If you are currently "in love."
12. If you are terrified of speaking in public.
13. If you secretly read the supermarket tabloids while waiting in the check-out line.
14. If you would like to bungee jump.
15. If you think there is intelligent life on other planets.
16. If you like liver and onions.
17. If you watch TV daily or almost every day.
18. If you have read an entire book in the last month.
19. If you have never camped in a tent.
20. If you enjoy professional wrestling.

Sit Down

Instructions to Leaders:

- This game is excellent for medium- to large-sized groups (40–100+ individuals).
- While this game doesn't call for any one-on-one interaction, it does allow people the opportunity to identify others in the room with similar (and/or unusual) interests and experiences and may pave the way for later conversation.
- This game requires no advance preparation.

Here's how it works:

Instruct everyone to stand before you begin. Have individuals sit down (and remain seated) when any statement is true of them.

The last person standing is the winner.

If everyone sits down before you get through the list, have everyone get back on their feet and continue reading the statements.

Sit Down . . .

1. If you know someone who served in Operation Desert Storm or Desert Shield.
2. If you have been to an opera.
3. If you have been to Niagara Falls.
4. If you are an only child.
5. If you are a twin.
6. If you know how to play the drums.
7. If you have received a speeding ticket.
8. If you have been on TV or the radio.
9. If you have attended an Olympic Games competition.
10. If you have never been to a professional sports event.
11. If you usually fail to wear your seat belt.
12. If you have traveled overseas.
13. If you know how to juggle.
14. If you were born in another country.
15. If you plan to get more than an undergraduate college degree.
16. If you would like to be a politician.
17. If you have never owned a dog.
18. If you like math.
19. If you have never had a cavity.
20. If you can barefoot water ski.

Sit Down . . . Again!

Instructions to Leaders:

■ This game is excellent for medium- to large-sized groups (40–100+people).
■ While this game doesn't call for any one-on-one interaction, it does allow participants a chance to identify others in the room with similar (and/or unusual) interests and experiences and may pave the way for later conversation.
■ This game requires no advance preparation.

Here's how it works:

Instruct everyone to stand before you begin. Have people sit down (and remain seated) when any statement is true of them.

The last person standing is the winner.

If everyone sits down before you get through the list, have everyone get back on their feet and continue reading the statements.

Sit Down . . .

1. If you forgot to put on deodorant today.
2. If you have read *War and Peace*.
3. If you have been skydiving.
4. If you have changed a diaper in the last month.
5. If you have totaled a car.
6. If you have been to Russia.
7. If you plan a career in professional sports.
8. If you got angry in traffic on the way here.
9. If you have cried at a movie in the last six months.
10. If you believe in UFOs.
11. If you like cats more than dogs.
12. If you think there are too many sports events on TV.
13. If you know how to ride a unicycle.
14. If you have been in this group for more than three years.
15. If you would like to be an astronaut.
16. If you are not wearing socks.
17. If you have skinny-dipped.
18. If you have ever made straight A's.
19. If you have never been hospitalized.
20. If you like foreign films.

Stand Up

Instructions to Leaders:

■ This game, like the Sit Down games, is excellent for medium- to large-sized groups (40–100+ participants).
■ While this game doesn't call for any one-on-one interaction, it does allow people to identify others in the room with similar (and/or unusual) interests and experiences and may pave the way for later conversation.
■ This game requires no advance preparation.

Here's how it works:

Instruct people to stand whenever any statement you read is true of them.

The last person sitting is the winner (or the most boring person—depending on how you want to look at it!).

If everyone stands before you get through the list, have everyone sit down again and continue reading the statements.

Stand Up . . .

1. If you have been in a major motion picture.
2. If you have run a marathon.
3. If you have more than $20 on you right now.
4. If you have your own car.
5. If you have ever been sent to the principal's or disciplinarian's office.
6. If you secretly are attracted to someone in this room.
7. If you think Lee Harvey Oswald acted alone in killing President John F. Kennedy.
8. If you have been interviewed for a TV news broadcast.
9. If you wear contact lenses.
10. If your cooking has set off a smoke alarm.
11. If you have never ridden a horse.
12. If you roll down the window and moo when you pass a herd of cows.
13. If you always carry a tissue or hankie.
14. If you would rather live somewhere else.
15. If you have never ridden on a motorcycle.
16. If you have never played a lottery game.
17. If you don't like pizza.
18. If you did *not* grow up watching *Sesame Street*.
19. If you sing in the shower.
20. If you are tired of this game.

Stand Up 2

Instructions to Leaders:

■ This game, like Stand Up, is excellent for medium- to large-sized groups (40–100+ individuals).

■ While this mixer doesn't call for any one-on-one interaction, it does allow people to identify others in the room with similar (and/or unusual) interests and experiences and may pave the way for later conversation.

■ This game requires no advance preparation.

Here's how it works:

Instruct everyone to sit down to begin the game. Have everyone stand (and remain standing) when any statement is true of them.

The last person still sitting is the winner.

If everyone stands before you get through the list, have everyone sit down again and continue reading the statements.

Stand Up . . .

1. If you ever ate dirt as a little kid.
2. If you are a sucker for door-to-door salesmen.
3. If you hate cats.
4. If you have ever shot a deer.
5. If you are a vegetarian.
6. If you don't know how to swim.
7. If you have had CPR training.
8. If you watch *less than* two hours of TV a week.
9. If you do aerobic exercise at least three times a week.
10. If you get scared in cemeteries.
11. If people say you have an unusual laugh.
12. If you have Native American descendants.
13. If you can play the saxophone.
14. If you request butter on your popcorn at the movies.
15. If you have ever used a tanning bed.
16. If you would consider plastic surgery.
17. If you think you'll have more than three kids.
18. If you like classical music.
19. If you have eaten sauerkraut in the last month.
20. If you snore.

Yes-No-Maybe

Instructions to Leaders:

■ This game is excellent for medium-sized groups (30–60 people).
■ While this mixer doesn't call for any one-on-one interaction, it does allow folks to identify others in the room with similar (and/or unusual) values and beliefs and may pave the way for later conversation.
■ This game requires minimal advance preparation—making three signs reading *YES, NO,* and *MAYBE* and posting these at the front of the room. (Put *MAYBE* in the middle.)

Here's how it works:

Have everyone stand in the front of the room. Tell the group that you will read a series of scenarios. People are to go and stand underneath the appropriate sign (i.e., that sign which indicates how they would react in each situation). After reading each situation, pause to allow everyone to find a place to stand.

I would yell at a basketball referee if I thought he or she made a bad call.
I would get angry if I arrived at the movies too late to see the previews.
I would tell a friend that he/she has bad breath.
I would cover my eyes in a scary movie.
I would be embarrassed if the topic of sex came up in mixed company.
I would go on a blind date.
I would tell someone to put out his or her cigarette if that person were smoking in a
    no-smoking section.
I would stop and ask directions if I were lost.
I would lie about my age.
I would take my own refreshments into a movie.
I would ask a waitress or waiter to take away my cold food and to bring me food that
    is hot.
I would walk out of a bad or offensive movie.

Celebrity Hunt

Instructions to Leaders:

■ This game works best with close-knit groups ranging from 25–50 people.
■ No advance preparation is required.

Here's how to explain this mixer to your group:

Give everyone a 4 X 6 index card and a pencil/pen. Instruct them to mill around the room, greeting each other and observing each other's appearances, mannerisms, etc.
   Tell people that they are to pick out three individuals in the room, who, in their opinion, most resemble famous celebrities (athletes, actors, musicians, politicians, etc.). Have everyone take notes on their cards. After five minutes, have a time of sharing.

Note: Be sure to urge people to be kind in their comparisons. Otherwise this surprisingly fun game can quickly turn cruel.

Brush with Greatness

Instructions to Leaders:

■ This game, based on a regular segment from the TV show *Late Night with David Letterman*, works best with small- to medium-sized groups who are *not* well-acquainted.
■ No advance preparation is required.

Here's how to explain this mixer to your group:

Give everyone a 4 X 6 index card and a pencil/pen. Instruct people to quietly write down an incident from their life in which they had a "brush with greatness" (that is, an encounter with someone famous).
   A sample "brush with greatness" goes like this:
   "I once met Jay Leno in the Dallas airport and I got his autograph on a five-dollar bill."
   After about five minutes, instruct everyone to finish up, to write their names on their cards, to fold the cards, and to turn them in.
   Tell the audience that you will read the cards one at a time, and they are to try to guess the person who had that experience.

Map of My Life *

Instructions to Leaders:

■ This mixer encourages interaction and understanding by allowing people to (a) show on a map the various places they have lived and (b) share personal insights that relate to each place from their past.
■ You will need to have one atlas or map for each small group doing this exercise.
■ This game can go for as long as you like, depending on the amount of detail you ask for.

Here's how it works:

Divide your group into small groups of no more than 12 individuals each. Give each small group a national map or atlas. The more detailed the map, the better.

Beginning with the oldest person present, have each individual walk the rest of the group through his or her life. In addition to pointing out the places on a map for the group to see, have each person share an interesting fact or story from each geographical location.

A sample "Map of My Life" tour would sound like this:

"I was born in Atlanta, Georgia. My dad was playing third base for the Atlanta Braves at the time. We lived there for two years. Then he was traded to the California Angels. So we moved way out to Anaheim. While there, my dad hurt his knee and retired from baseball. Then, when I was six, we moved to Dallas where my dad took a job with a real estate firm. We stayed there until I was in the tenth grade. Then we moved here to Tampa Bay."

*This mixer was created by Bret Hinkie, Minister to Youth at Christ Community Church in Ruston, LA.

John Hancock

Instructions to Leaders:

■ This mixer takes its name from the historical event in which American patriot John Hancock proudly signed the Declaration of Independence in big, bold letters.
■ Use this mixer with any size group to encourage people to greet each other and find out some basic information.
■ Play until someone completes the sheet or until five minutes are up.

Here's how it works:

1. Give everyone a copy of the statements below.
2. Instruct group members to move about the room and get autographs next to each of the statements below.
3. A person may sign next to a statement only if that statement is true of him or her.
4. Each person may sign another's sheet only once.
5. When anyone gets an autograph by all of the statements, he or she is to yell, "John Hancock! John Hancock!"

COVER THE INSTRUCTIONS ABOVE THIS LINE BEFORE PHOTOCOPYING THIS HANDOUT FOR YOUR GROUP.

- -

John Hancock

Quickly move about the room and find individuals who fit each of the following descriptions. When a statement is true of someone, he or she is to sign out to the right of it.

Note: Others may sign your sheet only once. You may sign others' sheets only once.

I enjoy eating frog legs:

I have been to the Eiffel Tower:

I have never had a cavity:

I enjoy playing/watching soccer:

I have never changed a flat tire:

I have snorkeled:

I am available for a dating relationship:

I bite my fingernails:

I have worked at a fast food restaurant:

I have called 9-1-1:

Eureka!

Instructions to Leaders:

■ This mixer works exactly like the previous one.
■ Use it with any size group to encourage people to greet each other and exchange interesting personal information.
■ Play until someone completes the sheet or until five minutes are up.

Here's how it works:

1. Give everyone a copy of the statements below.
2. Instruct people to move about the room and get autographs next to each of the statements below.
3. A person may sign next to a statement only if that statement is true of him or her.
4. Each person may sign another's sheet only once.
5. When anyone gets autographs for all of the statements, he or she is to yell "Eureka! Eureka!"

COVER THE INSTRUCTIONS ABOVE THIS LINE BEFORE PHOTOCOPYING THIS HANDOUT FOR YOUR GROUP.

- -

Eureka!

*Quickly move about the room and find individuals who fit each
of the following descriptions. When a statement is true of someone,
he or she is to sign out to the right of it.*

Note: Others may sign your sheet only once. You may sign others' sheets only once.

Someone whose last name begins with the letter "S":

A female with blue eyes:

Someone with a December birthday:

Someone who plays the piano:

A female with a gorgeous smile:

Someone who has let the air out of another's tires:

A male with dimples:

Someone under five foot two inches tall:

A former Boy Scout or Girl Scout:

Someone who has been swimming in the Great Salt Lake:

Medical Mixer

Instructions to Leaders:

■ This mixer works exactly like the previous two examples.
■ Use this mixer with any size group to encourage folks to meet and greet each other.
■ Play until someone completes the sheet or until five minutes are up.

■ Here's how it works:

1. Give everyone a copy of the statements below.
2. Tell everyone to move about the room and get different initials by each of the statements below.
3. A person may sign next to a statement only if that statement is true of him or her.
4. Each person may initial another's sheet only once.
5. The person who gets initials by all the statements first wins!

COVER THE INSTRUCTIONS ABOVE THIS LINE BEFORE PHOTOCOPYING THIS HANDOUT FOR YOUR GROUP.

- -

Medical Mixer

*Quickly move about the room and find individuals who fit each
of the following descriptions. When a statement is true of someone,
he or she is to initial out to the right of it.
Note: Players may sign another's sheet only once.*

Someone who is taking some form of medication:

Someone who has been to an emergency room in the last 12 months:

A person who takes vitamins regularly:

A person who can cough authentically:

Someone who is missing an appendix, tonsils, or wisdom teeth:

A person who wears glasses or contacts:

Someone with a bandaid somewhere on his or her body:

Someone who gargles on a regular basis:

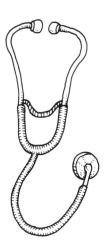

Medical Mixer 2

Instructions to Leaders:

■ Use this mixer with any size group to encourage folks to meet and greet each other.
■ Play until someone completes the sheet or until five minutes are up.

Here's how it works:

1. Give everyone a copy of the sheet below.
2. Instruct people to move about the room and get initials by each of the statements below.
3. A person may sign next to a statement only if that statement is true of him or her.
4. Each person may initial another's sheet only once.
5. The person who gets initials by all the statements first wins!

COVER THE INSTRUCTIONS ABOVE THIS LINE BEFORE PHOTOCOPYING THIS HANDOUT FOR YOUR GROUP.

- -

Medical Mixer 2

*Quickly move about the room and find individuals who fit each
of the following descriptions. When a statement is true of someone,
he or she is to initial out to the right of it.
Note: Players may sign another's sheet only once.*

Someone who has never broken a bone:

Someone who can tell you what the spleen does:

Someone who watches *General Hospital*:

Someone who plans a career in the medical profession:

Someone who has been hospitalized in the last five years:

Someone who thinks that doctors make too much money:

Someone who has had emergency surgery:

Someone who regularly gives blood:

Someone who hates going to the doctor:

Someone who had or has braces (dental):

Hobby Hunt

Instructions to Leaders:

- Use this mixer with any size group to encourage people to meet and find out a few basic facts about each other.
- Play until someone completes the sheet or until five minutes are up.

Here's how it works:

1. Give everyone a copy of the statements below.
2. Tell everyone to move about the room and get signatures by each of the statements below.
3. A person may sign next to a statement only if that statement is true of him or her.
4. Each person may sign another's sheet only once.
5. The person who gets signatures by all the statements first wins!

COVER THE INSTRUCTIONS ABOVE THIS LINE BEFORE PHOTOCOPYING THIS HANDOUT FOR YOUR GROUP.

- -

Hobby Hunt

*Quickly move about the room and find individuals who fit each
of the following descriptions. When a statement is true of someone,
he or she is to sign out to the right of it.
Note: Players may sign another's sheet only once.*

I collect something (for example, coins, stamps, baseball cards, etc.):

I am a regular jogger/runner:

I like to watch movies (either on video or on the big screen):

I enjoy painting or sculpting:

I would like to try scuba diving, sky diving, or hang gliding:

I knit, crochet, or needlepoint:

I enjoy working with wood:

I play golf or tennis:

My friends would say my chief hobby is guy-watching/girl-watching:

I have a hobby that many people would consider strange:

People Points

Instructions to Leaders:

- Use this mixer with any size group to encourage people to greet each other.
- Play until someone completes the sheet or until five minutes are up.

Here's how it works:

1. Give everyone a copy of the sheet below.
2. Have group members move about the room and get initials by each of the statements below.
3. A person may sign next to a statement only if that statement is true of him or her.
4. Each person may initial another's sheet only once.
5. The person who gets initials by all the statements first wins!
6. When time is called, add up your points (i.e., the total of the numbers in parentheses).

COVER THE INSTRUCTIONS ABOVE THIS LINE BEFORE PHOTOCOPYING THIS HANDOUT FOR YOUR GROUP.

- -

People Points

*You have five minutes to accumulate as many points as possible
by getting the initials of people who fit the following characteristics.
(The number of points follows each description):*

Someone wearing a bandaid (20):
Someone with a coin dated before 1965 on them (48):
Someone with a movie ticket stub on them (26):
Someone who celebrates a birthday this month (19):
Someone who will graduate this year (23):
Someone who is from out-of-state (13):
Someone who likes pimento-cheese sandwiches (29):
Someone who has been duck hunting (25):
Someone who has been to Australia (38):
Someone who has been (or will go) to college overseas (22):
Someone with a scar longer than two inches (30):
Someone who has bungee jumped (99):
Someone who plays the lottery (10):
Someone who has eaten snake (58):
Someone who can ride a unicycle (60):
Someone who has touched a stingray (27):
Someone with more than six siblings (45):
Someone who can speak German fluently (80):
Someone who enjoys "Calvin & Hobbes" (12):
Someone who has been treated for rabies (119):
Someone who has been to South America (77):

The One-to-Ten Game

Instructions to Leaders:

■ Use this mixer with any size group to encourage people to greet each other.
■ Play until someone completes the sheet or until five minutes are up.
■ For extra incentive, give a prize to the winner.

Here's how it works:

1. Give everyone a copy of the sheet below.
2. Have your group members move about the room and get signed statements by each of the numbers below.
3. A person may make only true statements.
4. Each person may sign another's sheet only once.
5. The first person to get ten statements and signatures wins.

COVER THE INSTRUCTIONS ABOVE THIS LINE BEFORE PHOTOCOPYING THIS HANDOUT FOR YOUR GROUP.

- -

The One-to-Ten Game

*Find ten different people who can each make a truthful statement about one
of the numbers from 1 to 10. Have these individuals write their name
and the statement that is true of them on your game sheet.
For example: Bill—I have only* **one** *kidney; Sue—I've shaken hands
with* **two** *U.S. Presidents; Tom—I have flunked algebra* **three** *times; etc.*

 1.

 2

 3

 4

 5

 6

 7

 8

 9

 10

Body Beautiful

Instructions to Leaders:

■ Use this mixer with any size group to encourage your group members to meet and find out a few basic facts about each other.
■ Play until someone completes the sheet or until five minutes are up.

Here's how it works:

1. Give everyone a copy of the game sheet below.
2. Instruct everyone to move about the room and get signatures by each of the statements below.
3. A person may sign next to a statement only if that statement is true of him or her.
4. Each person may sign another's sheet only once.
5. The first person to get a signature by each statement wins!

COVER THE INSTRUCTIONS ABOVE THIS LINE BEFORE PHOTOCOPYING THIS HANDOUT FOR YOUR GROUP.

- -

Body Beautiful

*Quickly move about the room and find individuals who truthfully
sign by each of the following descriptions.
Note: Do not let the same person sign more than once!*

I have blue eyes:

I have a dimple:

I am over six feet tall:

I have dieted in the last year:

I have ridden an exercise bike in the last year:

I watch body-building competitions on television:

I wish I could gain some weight:

I have a birthmark:

I work on my tan whenever possible:

Sports Spectacular

Instructions to Leaders:

■ Use this mixer with any size group to encourage folks to meet and find out a few basic facts about each other.
■ Play until someone completes the sheet or until five minutes are up.

Here's how it works:

1. Give everyone a copy of the statements below.
2. The goal is for people to get signatures by each of the statements below.
3. A person may sign next to a statement only if that statement is true of him or her.
4. Each person may sign another's sheet only once.
5. Whoever gets a signature by all the statements first wins!

COVER THE INSTRUCTIONS ABOVE THIS LINE BEFORE PHOTOCOPYING THIS HANDOUT FOR YOUR GROUP.
- -

Sports Spectacular

Quickly find individuals who can truthfully initial the following descriptions.
Note: Others may sign your sheet only once.
You may sign another person's sheet only once.

I have experience as an archer:

I can swim a mile or more without stopping:

I can do a flip off a diving board:

I think bowling should be banned from television:

I have messed up a knee playing competitive sports:

I have made a birdie playing golf:

I play tennis regularly:

I have suffered from shin splints:

I like to watch football:

I enjoy easygoing sports like horseshoes and ping-pong:

People Bingo

Instructions to Leaders:

■ Use this mixer with any size group to encourage folks to meet and find out a few basic facts about each other.
■ The goal is to get four signatures in a row either across, up and down, or diagonally.

Here's how it works:

1. Give everyone a copy of the "bingo" sheet below.
2. Have people move about the room and try to get four signatures in a row either across, up and down, or diagonally.
3. A person may sign a box only if that statement is true of him or her.
4. Each person may sign another's sheet only once.
5. Whoever gets four signatures in a row first (across, up and down, or diagonally) yells "Bingo!" and wins.

COVER THE INSTRUCTIONS ABOVE THIS LINE BEFORE PHOTOCOPYING THIS HANDOUT FOR YOUR GROUP.

People Bingo

Attempt to get individuals to sign a box containing a description that truthfully describes him or her. The first person to get four signatures in a row (across, up and down, or diagonally) wins! Note: No one may sign a sheet more than once.

I wish I had a breath freshener right now.	I am nice looking, but not conceited.	I am going to be famous one day.	I am afraid of the dark.
I am crazy about someone in this room.	I sweat a lot.	I wish my voice were deeper.	I think school is a waste of time.
The opposite sex finds me attractive.	I have made straight A's.	I have a nice singing voice.	I have big plans for the future.
The last date I went on was really terrible.	I have athlete's foot.	I sometimes pick my nose.	My brother/sister is a real pain in the neck.

People Bingo—The Sequel

Instructions to Leaders:

■ Use this mixer with any size group to encourage people to meet and learn a few basic facts about each other.
■ Play until someone has four signatures in a row (across, up and down, or diagonally).

Here's how it works:

1. Give everyone a copy of the statements below.
2. Encourage folks to move about the room and try to get four signatures in a row either across, up and down, or diagonally.
3. A person may sign a box only if that statement is true of him or her.
4. Each person may sign another's sheet only once.
5. When anyone gets four signatures in a row (across, up and down, or diagonally) he or she yells "Bingo!" and wins.

COVER THE INSTRUCTIONS ABOVE THIS LINE BEFORE PHOTOCOPYING THIS HANDOUT FOR YOUR GROUP.

- -

People Bingo—The Sequel

Attempt to get individuals to sign a box containing a description that truthfully describes him or her. The first person to get four signatures in a row (across, up and down, or diagonally) wins! Note: No one may sign a sheet more than once.

I can impersonate someone famous.	I read food labels.	I choose products primarily on the basis of cost.	I would sing a solo in a crowded fast food restaurant for $100.
Not all of my teeth are real.	I can roll my tongue.	I have a checking account.	I'd like to be a dog for one day.
I think teachers are underpaid and underappreciated.	I have been to a garage sale.	I can type more than 50 words a minute.	I am allergic to some type of food.
My weekend plans are looking good.	I clip coupons.	I prefer science over math.	I would like to learn to fly an airplane.

Retreat Roundup

Instructions to Leaders:

■ Use this mixer prior to a weekend retreat:
  (1) To allow people to meet and find out a few basic facts about each other; and
  (2) To promote the event and encourage sign-ups.
■ Play until someone has completed the sheet or until time is up.

Here's how it works:

1. Give everyone a copy of the mixer below.
2. Have everyone move about the room and try to get signatures next to each of the statements/descriptions.
3. A person may sign a line only if that statement is true of him or her.
4. Each person may sign another's sheet only once.
5. The first person to complete his or her sheet or to get the most signatures during the allotted time wins.

COVER THE INSTRUCTIONS ABOVE THIS LINE BEFORE PHOTOCOPYING THIS HANDOUT FOR YOUR GROUP.

- -

Retreat Roundup

Get signatures from the following folks.
Note: No one may sign a sheet more than once.

Someone who is *definitely* going on the upcoming retreat:

Someone who is *seriously considering* going on the upcoming retreat:

A person who has never been on a weekend retreat:

A person who attended our last retreat:

A person who can tell you three facts about the retreat agenda:

Someone who likes retreat food:

A person who knows the name of the retreat facility where we'll be staying:

Someone who needs a break from his or her family:

A person who has sung "Kum Ba Yah" around a campfire:

Someone who likes black and burnt-to-a-crisp marshmallows:

Spring Fever

Instructions to Leaders:

■ Use this mixer near the end of winter.
■ Use this mixer to give people an opportunity to meet and find out a few basic facts about each other.
■ Play until someone has completed his or her sheet or until time is up.

Here's how it works:

1. Give everyone a copy of the mixer below.
2. Encourage your group members to move about the room and try to get initials for each of the descriptions.
3. A person may initial only a statement that is true of him or her.
4. Each person may initial another's sheet only once.
5. The first person to complete his or her sheet or to get the most signatures during the allotted time wins.

COVER THE INSTRUCTIONS ABOVE THIS LINE BEFORE PHOTOCOPYING THIS HANDOUT FOR YOUR GROUP.

- -

Spring Fever

Attempt to get initials from the following folks.
Note: No one may initial a sheet more than once.

Someone who suffers from allergies:

Someone who is planning a trip to the beach during spring break:

A person who has already been working on his or her tan:

A person who is dreading having to work in the yard:

A person who can't wait for baseball to begin:

Someone who likes the smell of cut grass:

A person who will be doing some major spring cleaning:

Someone who will miss the cold weather:

A person who has already been shopping for new clothes:

Someone who will be wearing a new swimsuit this season:

Summer Survey

Instructions to Leaders:

■ Use this mixer at the end of spring or beginning of summer.
■ Use this mixer to give folks an opportunity to be a little crazy as well as to meet others.
■ Play until someone has completed his or her sheet or until time is up.

Here's how it works:

1. Give everyone a copy of the mixer below.
2. Have everyone work his or her way through the following list of instructions as quickly as possible.
3. The first person to complete his or her sheet or to get the most initials during the allotted time wins.

COVER THE INSTRUCTIONS ABOVE THIS LINE BEFORE PHOTOCOPYING THIS HANDOUT FOR YOUR GROUP.

- -

Summer Survey

Quickly work your way through the following list of instructions:

■ Compare your tan with the darkest or fairest-skinned person in the room. He or she signs here:

■ Take 15 seconds to tell someone your summer plans. That person signs here:

■ Ask three people if they have seen your rubber duckie. The third signs here:

■ Tell someone this joke and then fall on the ground laughing hysterically:

> *"Last summer where I was it got so hot
> the cows were giving evaporated milk!"*

Get your witness to sign here:

■ "Dog paddle" to the front of the room and back. Get a witness to sign here:

■ Get with someone else and sing the chorus to a Beach Boys song. Your partner signs here:

■ Get the signature of someone you probably won't see until September:

Back-to-School Bash

Instructions to Leaders:

■ Use this mixer a week or two into a new school term.
■ This mixer is ideal for people who need to get reacquainted.
■ Play until someone has completed his or her sheet or until time is up.

Here's how it works:

1. Give everyone a copy of the mixer below.
2. Tell people to find others who can truthfully initial the statements listed below.
3. They are permitted only one signature from each individual per sheet.
4. The first person to complete his or her sheet or to get the most signatures during the allotted time wins.

- -

Back-to-School Bash

Quickly find others who can truthfully initial the statements listed below.
Only one signature from each individual per sheet.

■ Someone who has already been lost looking for a class:

■ A person who has checked out a book from the school library:

■ Someone who has cleaned his or her plate in the cafeteria:

■ A person who has accidentally gone into the wrong rest room:

■ A person who has been late to at least three classes:

■ Someone who has already been absent:

■ A person who "chauffeurs" someone else to school:

■ A person who had (or has) trouble getting their locker open:

■ Someone who has yet to do any homework:

■ Someone who has already done something embarrassing at school this year:

■ A person who brings a sack lunch:

Fall Frenzy

Instructions to Leaders:

■ Use this mixer in early fall when the leaves and weather first begin to change.
■ Use it to give group members unusual insights into each other.
■ Play until someone has completed their sheet or until time is up.

Here's how it works:

1. Give everyone a copy of the game sheet below.
2. Have folks locate others who can truthfully initial each of the statements.
3. Only one signature from each individual is allowed per sheet.
4. The first person to complete his or her sheet or to get the most signatures during the allotted time wins.

COVER THE INSTRUCTIONS ABOVE THIS LINE BEFORE PHOTOCOPYING THIS HANDOUT FOR YOUR GROUP.

- -

Fall Frenzy

*Quickly find others who can truthfully initial the statements listed below.
Only one signature from each individual is permitted per sheet.*

■ Someone who is dreading having to rake leaves:

■ A person who prefers cold weather over hot:

■ Someone who has purchased a new sweater in the last month:

■ A person who plans to see a college or professional football game in person this fall:

■ A person who thinks that most of the new fall TV shows are stupid:

■ Someone who can't wait to build a fire in the fireplace:

■ A person who is enjoying school so far this year:

■ A person who wonders why they play baseball all the way into October:

■ Someone who has eaten oatmeal, grits, or Cream of Wheat for breakfast this week:

■ Someone who has already started his or her Christmas shopping:

Thanksgiving Mixer

Instructions to Leaders:

- Use this mixer as the Thanksgiving holiday approaches.
- Use it to give people an opportunity to interact with three other individuals.
- Allow the groups to visit for five to seven minutes.
- For extra fun, have the best turkey impersonators from each group do a "gobble off" for the whole group.

Here's how it works:

Give everyone a copy of the statements and questions below.

COVER THE INSTRUCTIONS ABOVE THIS LINE BEFORE PHOTOCOPYING THIS HANDOUT FOR YOUR GROUP.

Thanksgiving Mixer

Find three other people and sit down together. Work your way through the following questions/statements, beginning with the person who looks most like a pilgrim

- What things/people/blessings are you most grateful for right now?

- What are your plans for the Thanksgiving holiday?

- What is a typical Thanksgiving Day like in your home?

- Determine who in your group does the best turkey impersonation.

Season's Greetings

Instructions to Leaders:

■ Use this mixer at the beginning of the Christmas holidays.
■ Use it to give people an opportunity to be a little crazy as well as greet others.
■ Play until someone has completed his or her sheet or until time is up.

Here's how it works:

1. Give everyone a copy of the mixer below.
2. Tell participants to work their way through the following list of instructions as quickly as possible.
3. Whoever completes his or her sheet or gets the most initials during the allotted time wins the game.

- -

Season's Greetings

Quickly work your way through the following list of instructions.

■ Give someone a 15 second speech on "Why People Need To Drink More Eggnog." He or she signs here:
■ Tell someone this riddle then fall on the floor laughing hysterically.
Q: What goes "Ho-ho-ho . . . thud"?
A: Santa Claus, laughing his head off!
That person signs here:
■ Get together with eight other people. Have one person play Santa Claus (saying, "Ho-ho-ho" etc.) and the rest impersonate reindeer (snorting, stomping, etc.) The reindeer should then pick up Santa and parade him or her around the room. Have a team member initial here:
■ Get together with three other folks and sing "Deck the Halls." Get one of those folks to sign here:
■ Sit in someone's lap and tell him or her what you want for Christmas. Get your "Santa" to sign right here:
■ Find a partner and "snow ski" together across the room and back. Your partner signs here:
■ Do your best "Grinch" impersonation. Get a witness to sign here:
■ Find two others and dance like the Peanuts cartoon characters do on the TV special "A Charlie Brown Christmas." One of them signs here:

Christmas Confusion

Instructions to Leaders:

■ Use this mixer during the Christmas holidays (it is ideal for Christmas parties).
■ Use it to give people an opportunity to meet someone new and greet someone old.
■ Play until someone has completed his or her sheet or until time is up.

Here's how it works:

1. Give everyone a copy of the game sheet below.
2. Have participants find others who can truthfully autograph the statements.
3. Only one signature from each individual is allowed per sheet.
4. The first person to complete his or her sheet or to get the most signatures during the allotted time wins.

COVER THE INSTRUCTIONS ABOVE THIS LINE BEFORE PHOTOCOPYING THIS HANDOUT FOR YOUR GROUP.

Christmas Confusion

Quickly find others who can truthfully sign the statements listed below.
Only one signature from each individual is allowed per sheet.

■ Someone who has never received a bike for Christmas:

■ A person who has spent Christmas in a foreign country:

■ Someone who actually *likes* fruitcake:

■ Someone who is planning to snow ski this winter:

■ A person who has never seen the holiday movie classic, *It's a Wonderful Life:*

■ Someone who plans to spend more than $200 on gifts this year:

■ A person who sends out Christmas cards:

■ A person who has already been to a Christmas pageant, play, or festival:

■ Someone who has seen an actual live reindeer:

■ Someone who has been called "Scrooge" or "The Grinch":

The Price Is Right

Instructions to Leaders:

■ This mixer will require some advance preparation—checking the prices of the items listed below.

■ Use this mixer before a meeting or discussion on the topics of "money" or "values."

■ Use it to give people an opportunity to interact with each other.

■ Allow the groups to visit for five to seven minutes.

■ Read the actual prices and let each group see how far they were off the mark.

Here's how it works:

Give everyone a copy of the statements and questions below.

COVER THE INSTRUCTIONS ABOVE THIS LINE BEFORE PHOTOCOPYING THIS HANDOUT FOR YOUR GROUP.

- -

The Price Is Right

Find three other people and sit down together. After exchanging names and the name of one material possession you don't have but would like to own, try to agree together on the current retail price of the following items.

■ A brand-new Toyota pick-up (basic model):

■ A box of Cheerios:

■ A sunroof installed in your car:

■ Dinner for two at the nicest restaurant in town:

■ A five pound bag of sugar:

■ Round trip ticket from New York to London on Delta airlines:

■ A pound of ground beef:

■ Beginner piano lessons (per half hour):

Part Two:

MIXING & MINGLING

Dragnet

Instructions to Leaders:

■ Use this mixer to give folks an opportunity to interact with each other on a deeper level.

■ Allow your group to mix and mingle for five to seven minutes.

Here's how it works:

1. Give everyone a copy of the statements and questions below.
2. Have each person find a partner and begin working through the instructions.

- - - - - - - - - - - - COVER THE INSTRUCTIONS ABOVE THIS LINE BEFORE PHOTOCOPYING THIS HANDOUT FOR YOUR GROUP. - - - - - - - - - - - - - -

 Dragnet

Hook up with another "detective" and together work your way through this list.
You have seven minutes to uncover as many facts as possible.

■ Meet another pair and discover who has the most distinguished-sounding full name.

■ Corral another twosome and find out who has the weirdest food fixation (for example, ketchup on ice cream, etc.).

■ Grab a third couple and see where everyone was born.

■ Stop a fourth pair and determine each others' political views.

■ Greet another detective team and find out who is the best driver (that is, who has the fewest tickets, wrecks, etc.).

■ Locate another couple and ascertain each others' hobbies.

■ Find another pair of private investigators and discover each person's taste in music.

■ Pair up with a final twosome and quickly learn the *real* reason each person came to this meeting.

Twosomes

Instructions to Leaders:

■ Use this mixer to give participants an opportunity to interact with each other beyond a superficial level.
■ Allow the mixing and mingling to continue for at least five to seven minutes.

Here's how it works:

1. Give everyone a copy of the statements and questions below.
2. Tell everyone to find a partner and begin working their way through the instructions.

- -

Twosomes

Pair up with someone you know well or fairly well. Then together work your way through as many of these items as possible.

■ Talk with another pair about weekend plans.

■ Meet a couple who have taken a class together.

■ Talk with another twosome about some hot news item.

■ Chat with a fourth pair about the grossest school food you've ever seen.

■ Discuss your favorite aspect of this group with another couple.

■ With another twosome invent a new, outrageous, secret handshake.

■ Swap clean jokes with another pair of folks.

■ Form a circle with four other couples and do the "backrub thing."

■ Sing the chorus of a Top 40 song with two other pairs of folks.

The Interview

Instructions to Leaders:

■ Use this mixer to give individuals an opportunity to interact with one other person beyond a superficial level.

■ Allow the interviews to last for at least five minutes, but not more than ten minutes total.

■ When you're done, have volunteers share their findings with the group.

Here's how it works:

1. Give everyone a copy of the handout below.
2. Instruct participants to locate a partner and begin working through the exercise.

COVER THE INSTRUCTIONS ABOVE THIS LINE BEFORE PHOTOCOPYING THIS HANDOUT FOR YOUR GROUP.
- -

The Interview

(Find a partner and interview each other by asking the following questions.
Note: Take good notes—you may be asked to
report your findings to the group!)

1. Name:

2. Nickname:
   (if none now, one you had when younger)

3. Freakiest Food Fetish:
   (for example, honey, mustard, and tomato sandwich)

4. Weirdest Pet Story:
   (for example, "My cat named George once had kittens in our microwave oven.")

5. Biggest Honor You Have Received:

6. A Goal You Have:

"Get to Know Me!"

Instructions to Leaders:

■ Use this mixer to give individuals an opportunity to interact with three other people beyond a superfical level.
■ Allow folks five to seven minutes to complete this exercise.
■ When you're done, have volunteers share their findings with the group.

Here's how it works:

1. Give everyone a copy of the sheet below.
2. Encourage people to probe for really interesting details, things like "I once jumped out of tree and broke both arms," rather than "I have a brother named Bill."

COVER THE INSTRUCTIONS ABOVE THIS LINE BEFORE PHOTOCOPYING THIS HANDOUT FOR YOUR GROUP.

- -

"Get to Know Me!"

Meet three new people and find out one interesting, little-known fact about each.
Note: You will be asked to report your findings to the group!

■ Person #1:
   Amazing Fact:

■ Person #2:
   Amazing Fact:

■ Person #3:
   Amazing Fact:

Get Together

Instructions to Leaders:

■ Use this mixer to give group members an opportunity to interact with each other beyond a superficial level.

■ Allow the mixing and mingling to continue for five to ten minutes.

Here's how it works:

Give everyone a copy of the statements and questions below.

Get Together

*In the next five to ten minutes, complete at least five
of the following ten instructions.*

■ Get together with three other people wearing tennis shoes. Take turns sharing your names and favorite sports.

■ Get together with three other people who have lived out of state. Share your names and plans for the future.

■ Get together with two others who were in church Sunday and tell what part of the sermon you each enjoyed most.

■ Get together with someone your same age (within five years) and tell what you like best about living where you do.

■ Get together with someone wearing the same color shirt, and tell full names plus what you like best about this season of the year.

■ Get together with two others who plan to go on the next group trip or retreat and predict where we'll be going and what we'll be doing.

■ Get together with three others (so that you have two males and two females) and share what you feel are the primary differences between the sexes.

■ Get together with someone who has your own eye color and tell something interesting about your respective families.

■ Get together with two others who have eaten Mexican food this week and tell about the most famous person you have ever met.

■ Get together with someone you see on a daily basis and talk about the biggest trial you are currently facing.

True Stories

Instructions to Leaders:

■ Use this mixer to give people an opportunity to interact with each other, and to develop listening skills.
■ Allow the groups to visit for ten to twelve minutes.

Here's how it works:

1. Give everyone a copy of the instructions below.
2. Emphasize that everyone should get into groups of four and that the sharing should begin with the person who has read the most Shakespeare.

- -

True Stories

Find three other people and sit down together. Take turns telling the following stories, beginning with the person who has read the most Shakespeare.

Person #1—Briefly tell about the time you were most afraid.

Person #2—Briefly tell about the angriest you have ever been.

Person #3—Briefly tell about the best vacation you have ever taken.

Person #4—Briefly tell about the hardest you have ever laughed.

Famous Couples

Instructions to Leaders:

■ Use this mixer to give people an opportunity to have fun and interact with others.
■ Allow your group ten minutes to complete this exercise.

Here's how it works:

1. Mix up the following names, *making sure that you have one name for each person attending your meeting*, and *making sure that you give out both partners of each couple listed*. (You may wish to supplement the list below with some couples from your own church or group.)
2. Give each person at your meeting a name. At the signal, each person must walk around the room calling out the name of his or her match. For example, "Rhett Butler" calls out "Scarlett O'Hara" until he finds the person with that name (who happens to be calling out "Rhett Butler"). If you wish to make this game a bit more challenging, do not tell people who their match is. For example, a person with the name "Garth" would have to guess that "Garth" goes with "Wayne." He or she would then walk around calling out "Wayne."
3. When each couple is "reunited," they should chat briefly with the purpose of finding out a little bit about each other (such as name, place of birth, goal in life, etc.).

Roy Rogers/Dale Evans
Bill Clinton/Hillary Clinton
Dan Quayle/Marilyn Quayle
Lone Ranger/Tonto
Batman/Robin
Mickey Mouse/Minnie Mouse
Tarzan/Jane
Superman/Lois Lane
Abbott/Costello
Ronald Reagan/Nancy Reagan
Romeo/Juliet
Regis Philbin/Kathie Lee Gifford
Ricky Ricardo/Lucy Ricardo
Calvin/Hobbes
Frankenstein/Wolfman
Paul Simon/Art Garfunkel
King Kong/Fay Wray
Michael Jackson/Bubbles
George Burns/Gracie Allen
George Bush/Barbara Bush
Lewis/Clark
Sam Donaldson/Dianne Sawyer
Ham/Eggs
Shoes/Socks
Peanut Butter/Jelly
Hi/Lois

Wayne/Garth
Samson/Delilah
Tom/Jerry
Elliott/E.T.
Linus/Blanket
Andy Taylor/Barney Fife
Cream/Sugar
David Letterman/Paul Shaffer
Jerry Lewis/Dean Martin
Mark Antony/Cleopatra
Jim Bakker/Tammy Faye Bakker
Lassie/Timmy
Blondie/Dagwood
Fred Astaire/Ginger Rogers
Johnny Carson/Ed McMahon
Hall/Oates
Demi Moore/Bruce Willis
Laurel/Hardy
Hans Solo/Princess Leia
Mork/Mindy
Rogers/Hammerstein
Rhett Butler/Scarlett O'Hara
Salt/Pepper
Fork/Knife
Starsky/Hutch
Ruth/Boaz

Getting to Know You

Instructions to Leaders:

■ Use this mixer to give medium- to large-sized groups (25–60) an opportunity to interact with each other.
■ Allow your group to visit for ten to twelve minutes.
■ If you can find it on tape, the song "Getting to Know You" from the Broadway musical *The King and I* works well as background music. Or you can have a pianist play it while your group mingles. Or you can simply blow a whistle when people are supposed to stop greeting and begin interacting.

Here's how it works:

1. Tell everyone to move about the room shaking hands and greeting each other.
2. Explain that when they hear the music stop (or the whistle blow), they should pair off with the person whose hand they are shaking, or just dropped, or were about to shake and to take turns answering two questions.
3. For best results, use an overhead projector to flash the questions up on the wall.
4. Repeat this process four times.

QUESTIONS:

What is the best class you ever took and why?
Where would you like to vacation and why?

Who has had the biggest influence on your life and why?
What is the secret of happiness?

What is your favorite song and why?
What, in your opinion, is the coolest breed of dog?

What national/international problem would you most like to fix?
What is your favorite season and why?

Getting to Know You 2

Instructions to Leaders:

■ Use this mixer to give medium- to large-sized groups an opportunity to interact with each other.
■ Allow the groups to visit for ten to twelve minutes.
■ If you can find it on tape, the song "Getting to Know You" from the Broadway musical *The King and I* works well as background music. Or you can have a pianist play it while your group mingles. Or you can simply blow a whistle when people are supposed to stop greeting and begin interacting.

Here's how it works:

1. Tell everyone to move about the room shaking hands and greeting each other.
2. Explain that when they hear the music stop (or the whistle blow), they should pair off with the person whose hand they are shaking, or just dropped, or were about to shake and to take turns finishing two statements.
3. For best results, use an overhead projector to flash the statements up on the wall.
4. Repeat this process four times.

FINISH THE STATEMENTS:

My favorite zoo animal is:
A hobby I'd like to try is:

One of my goals for this year is:
The hardest class I've ever taken was/is:

The best movie I've seen this year is:
The most pain I've ever experienced was when:

The best pet I ever had was:
The person I respect most is (explain why too):

How's the W-E-A-T-H-E-R?

Instructions to Leaders:

■ This mixer is based on the concept that many people have difficulty talking about anything more personal than the weather.
■ Use it to give folks an opportunity to interact with each other, as well as to give them an acronym that can sharpen their communication skills.
■ Allow people to visit for ten to twelve minutes.

Here's how it works:

1. Organize everyone in groups of two, three, or four.
2. Have them converse based on the acronym W-E-A-T-H-E-R (you will probably want to write it on poster board, a marker board, or an overhead projector).

CONVERSATIONAL QUESTIONS:

Do you WORK? (If so, where? For how long?)

What kind of foods do you like to EAT?

What ACTIVITIES are you involved in—besides school and/or work?

Where would you like to TRAVEL and why?

Do you have any HOBBIES? If so, what?

What is your favorite way to EXERCISE?

What are the most important RELATIONSHIPS in your life and why?

Scavenger Hunt

Instructions to Leaders:

■ Use this mixer to help your group members gain unique insights into each other.
■ Play until someone has completed their sheet or until time is up.

Here's how it works:

1. Give everyone a copy of the game sheet below.
2. Instruct participants to find others who can truthfully initial the statements.
3. Individuals may initial a sheet only once.
4. Whoever completes his or her sheet first or gets the most initials during the allotted time wins.

COVER THE INSTRUCTIONS ABOVE THIS LINE BEFORE PHOTOCOPYING THIS HANDOUT FOR YOUR GROUP.

- -

Scavenger Hunt

Get the initials of individuals who fit the following characteristics.
Note: Items must be in this room!

■ Someone who has a picture of his or her mother:

■ A person with a calculator:

■ Someone with more than $1 in change:

■ Someone possessing food, gum, or candy:

■ A person who is not wearing socks:

■ Someone with more than eight items on his or her keychain:

■ A person with a wart:

■ A person carrying a toothbrush:

■ Someone with a scab:

■ Someone with a credit card:

Common Bond

Instructions to Leaders:

■ Use this mixer to help people gain unique information about each other.
■ Play until someone has completed his or her sheet or until time is up.

Here's how it works:

1. Give everyone a copy of the game sheet below.
2. Inform people to find others who can truthfully sign the statements.
3. Explain that individuals may sign a sheet only once.
4. The person completing his or her sheet first or getting the most signatures during the allotted time wins.

COVER THE INSTRUCTIONS ABOVE THIS LINE BEFORE PHOTOCOPYING THIS HANDOUT FOR YOUR GROUP.

- -

Common Bond

*Get the signatures of individuals who have the
following things in common with you.*

■ I share your birth *month*:

■ I am the same year in school as you:

■ I live in the same neighborhood:

■ I have similar tastes in music as you:

■ I have the same name (first, last, or middle):

■ I like the same kind of dessert:

■ I enjoy the same hobby or pastime:

■ I am in the same mood right now:
(happy, sad, laid back, apathetic, stressed, angry, etc.)

■ I have the same favorite color:

■ I read the same magazine(s) as you:

True Confessions

Instructions to Leaders:

■ Use this mixer to help your group members learn interesting facts about each other.
■ Play until someone has completed his or her sheet or until time is up.

Here's how it works:

1. Give everyone a copy of the game sheet below.
2. Tell people to find others who can truthfully initial the statements.
3. Explain that players may initial each sheet only once.
4. Whoever completes his or her sheet first or gets the most initials during the allotted time wins.

COVER THE INSTRUCTIONS ABOVE THIS LINE BEFORE PHOTOCOPYING THIS HANDOUT FOR YOUR GROUP.

- -

True Confessions

Get the initials of individuals who can truthfully
make the following confessions:

■ I have let the air out of someone's tires:

■ I shoplifted something as a little kid:

■ I am wild about someone in this room:

■ I have skinny-dipped:

■ I have stolen fruit or vegetables from a field or a fruit stand:

■ I have sneaked out of the house:

■ I enjoy reading tabloids like *The National Enquirer:*

■ I have made a prank telephone call in the last year:

Hidden Talents

Instructions to Leaders:

■ Use this mixer to help group members gain interesting insights into each other.
■ Play until someone has completed his or her sheet or until time is up.

Here's how it works:

1. Give everyone a copy of the game sheet below.
2. Instruct group members to find others who can truthfully sign next to the statements.
3. Participants may sign each sheet only once.
4. Whoever completes his or her sheet first or gets the most signatures during the allotted time wins.

COVER THE INSTRUCTIONS ABOVE THIS LINE BEFORE PHOTOCOPYING THIS HANDOUT FOR YOUR GROUP.

- -

Hidden Talents

Get an autograph from individuals who possess the following amazing abilities:

■ Someone who knows CPR or the Heimlich maneuver:

■ Someone who plays the guitar:

■ Someone who can touch his or her tongue to his or her own nose (must demonstrate):

■ Someone who can do a split (must demonstrate):

■ Someone who—standing and with legs straight—can touch his or her palms on the floor:

■ Someone who can wiggle his or her ears or nose (must demonstrate):

■ Someone who can juggle:

■ Someone who can imitate Donald Duck (must demonstrate):

■ Someone who can do a one-armed pushup (must demonstrate):

■ Someone who can do a backward flip off a diving board:

Secret Desires

Instructions to Leaders:

■ Use this mixer to help group members learn unknown facts about each other.
■ Play until someone has completed his or her sheet or until time is up.

Here's how it works:

1. Give everyone a copy of the game sheet below.
2. Players must find others who can truthfully sign the statements.
3. Participants may sign each sheet only once.
4. Whoever completes his or her sheet first or gets the most signatures during the allotted time wins.

- -

Secret Desires

Get autographs from individuals who possess the following secret hopes:

■ Someone who craves a career as a musician:

■ Someone who would like to write a book one day:

■ A person who would like to compete in a triathalon:

■ Someone who feels that he or she will earn a doctorate:

■ Someone who wishes to become famous:

■ A person who hopes for a career in law or politics:

■ Someone who wants a big family:

■ A person who would like to go out with someone else in this room:

■ Someone who dreams of a career as a professional athlete:

■ A person who wants to be a millionaire by age 40:

Fearsome Foursome

Instructions to Leaders:

■ Use this mixer to encourage deeper communication among your group members.
■ Allow interaction to continue for at least 10 minutes.

Here's how it works:

1. Give everyone a copy of the game sheet below, or give the instructions verbally one at a time.
2. Encourage participants to resist the urge to discuss other topics.
3. Use a watch with a second hand to insure that the time doesn't get away from you.

COVER THE INSTRUCTIONS ABOVE THIS LINE BEFORE PHOTOCOPYING THIS HANDOUT FOR YOUR GROUP.

- -

Fearsome Foursome

1. Get together with three other folks, find a spot on the floor, and sit down.

2. Take 30 seconds each to give your personal highlights and lowlights of the last month.

3. Take 20 seconds apiece to tell your plans for the upcoming weekend.

4. Take 15 seconds each describing the *perfect* weekend.

5. Take 10 seconds each to share an idea that would make this town/city a better place.

Ten Questions

Instructions to Leaders:

■ Use this mixer—a modified form of the old classic *Twenty Questions*—to encourage deeper communication among your group members.
■ Allow interaction to continue for about 10 minutes.

Here's how it works:

1. Give everyone a copy of the game sheet below, or give the instructions verbally one at a time.
2. Use a watch with a second hand to insure that the time doesn't get away from you.

COVER THE INSTRUCTIONS ABOVE THIS LINE BEFORE PHOTOCOPYING THIS HANDOUT FOR YOUR GROUP.

- -

Ten Questions

Instructions:

1. Grab a partner (someone you know well or fairly well).
2. Team up with another twosome that you *don't* know well or at all. (There should now be four people in your group.)
3. Beginning with the person in your foursome who has eaten fast food most recently, play "Ten Questions," a modified form of the game "Twenty Questions." [Remember in this game, only "yes" or "no" type questions are allowed!]
4. For player number one, the topic is "The Person (Living or Dead) You Most Admire."
5. After two minutes, time will be called, and your group will proceed to question player two (the person to the left of player one) using a new category (see below).
6. Continue in this manner until all four people in your group have been questioned.

Category for player #2: The Food that You Hate the Most

Category for player #3: A Wild Animal You Would Like to Trade Places with for One Day

Category for player #4: The Historical Event at Which You Would Most Like to Have Been Present

Favorite Things!

Instructions to Leaders:

■ Use this mixer, based on the song "My Favorite Things" from the popular Academy Award winning movie *The Sound of Music,* to encourage deeper communication among your group members.
■ Allow interaction to continue for about 10 minutes.

Here's how it works:

1. Divide into small groups of 6–10 people each.
2. Give everyone a copy of the game sheet below.
3. Use a watch with a second hand to insure that the time doesn't get away from you.

- -

Favorites Things!

After going around your small group and introducing yourselves, take **four** minutes to list quickly your favorite things on this sheet. Your list should list simple pleasures—things that make you smile.

A sample list might be: Oreos, the *USA Today,* fireplaces, fresh-cut Christmas trees, new tennis shoes, frosty mornings, naps on Sunday afternoon, etc.

When the time is up, take turns reading your lists aloud, beginning with the person who has seen *The Sound of Music* the most times. If someone else mentions a favorite thing that is on your list, circle that item, and write that person's initials next to it.

The goal is twofold: (1) to get to know each other a bit better; and (2) to see which group member(s) you have the most in common with.

 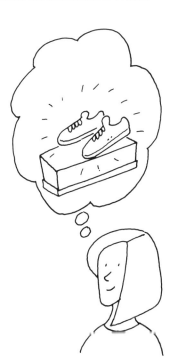 

I Predict

Instructions to Leaders:

■ Use this mixer in small groups to encourage deeper communication among your group members.

■ Allow interaction to continue for about 10 minutes.

Here's how it works:

1. Give everyone a copy of the game sheet below, or give the instructions verbally one at a time.

2. Use a watch with a second hand to insure that the time doesn't get away from you.

- -

I Predict

Get into groups of four—at least one member of the opposite sex per group—
and quickly give your predictions to the following questions.
Note: Each person must share at least two predictions with the group.

■ What person in this room will become the most successful and why?

■ What will our society be like in 10 years?

■ What will be the most amazing invention or scientific breakthrough in your lifetime?

■ What will be the next major news story or event to break?

■ Describe your life 15 years from right now (where you'll be, what you'll be doing, etc.)

Majority Rules

Instructions to Leaders:

■ This fun, mathematical, competitive mixer helps medium- to large-sized groups get better acquainted.
■ Allot at least 10 minutes for this exercise.

Here's how it works:

1. Instruct your group to form six teams based on the month in which they were born. People born in January or February are Team #1; those in March–April are Team #2; May–June babies are Team #3; those with July–August birthdates are Team #4; September–October folks are Team #5; and November–December babies are Team #6.
2. Have everyone mill about and locate their teams.
3. As teams begin to form, give each team a copy of the sheet below. It is self-explanatory.
4. When the sheets are turned in, average each team's percentages to get an overall average and determine the winning team.

- -

Majority Rules

After you have gathered all your members, answer the following questions and calculate your team's percentages. The only rule is that you must be honest!

Your team number: _____ The number of people on your team: _____

CATEGORY	PERCENTAGE
1. The number of people on your team who have been to a football game (in a stadium) in the last year:	
2. The number of people on your team who like anchovies:	
3. The number of people on your team who can roll their tongue into a U-shape:	
4. The number of people on your team who can say "I love you" in a foreign language:	
5. The number of people on your team who have more than $10 on them right now:	
6. The number of people on your team who would let a dog lick them on the mouth:	
7. The number of people on your team who talk and/or walk in their sleep:	
8. The number of people on your team who prefer Pepsi over Coke:	
9. The number of people on your team who have a CD player:	
10. The number of people on your team who have hitchhiked:	

(When you have calculated what percentage of your team falls into each category, turn this sheet in and we will determine which of the six teams has the best overall percentage.)

Creative Announcements

Instructions to Leaders:

■ This unique exercise not only helps promote your upcoming events, but it also gives groups a chance to mingle and see each other in a new light.
■ Plan on this taking at least 20 minutes.
■ Determine how many announcements you have and divide your group into that many smaller groups. Assign each group a specific announcement.
■ Then, having typed or written your specific announcements below, give each group a copy of the handout that follows:

COVER THE INSTRUCTIONS ABOVE THIS LINE BEFORE PHOTOCOPYING THIS HANDOUT FOR YOUR GROUP.

- -

Creative Announcements

Instructions:
1. Spend one minute having each person in your group tell his or her name and the person he or she most admires.
2. Have someone read the rest of this sheet aloud to the group.
3. Find your announcement in the list below and note its pertinent facts:

Group #1:   Group #2:
Group #3:   Group #4:
Group #5:   Group #6:

3. Decide on the most creative way to present your information to the group. Some suggestions are:

■ a quick skit	■ a rap	■ an impersonation of someone famous
■ singing the info to a familiar tune	■ charades	■ a monologue
■ a mock commercial	■ song & dance	■ a poem
■ a short speech	■ a choir number	■ a mock newscast
■ a mini-opera	■ a parody	■ a series of knock-knock jokes
■ lip-synch	■ a ballet	■ a vaudeville routine
■ mime	■ a role play	■ a series of puns & wordplays
■ modern dance	■ a fairy tale	■ a scene from a movie

4. Decide on the form your announcement will take.
5. Decide who will do what in your presentation.
6. Practice/rehearse.
7. Perform your announcement for the group.

Important Notes:
Be *friendly*! The first goal here is to meet someone new.
Be *creative*! The second goal here is to make these announcements as interesting as possible.
Be *quick*! There is no time to dilly-dally.
Be *fun*! Don't worry about acting silly. No one is videotaping us. No stories will appear in the local newspaper.

If I Were King/Queen

Instructions to Leaders:

■ This fun discussion mixer helps small- to medium-sized groups get better acquainted.
■ It takes about 10 minutes.
■ Use this mixer before a meeting on power or values.

Here's how it works:

1. Divide into groups of four to eight people each.
2. Give each person a copy of the sheet below. It is self-explanatory.

COVER THE INSTRUCTIONS ABOVE THIS LINE BEFORE PHOTOCOPYING THIS HANDOUT FOR YOUR GROUP.

- -

If I Were King/Queen

Take turns answering the following questions. Begin with the person who is the most knowledgeable about Britain's royal family.

If I were king/queen, I would concentrate on:
(name two or three issues)

If I were king/queen, I would solve the crime problem by:
(describe your strategy)

If I were king/queen, I would go on TV and say:
(summarize your message to the nation)

If I were king/queen, I would make the following changes in society:
(name three)

If I were king/queen, I would make the following changes in my personal life:
(list a couple)

Money Matters

Instructions to Leaders:

■ This fun discussion mixer helps small- to medium-sized groups get better acquainted.
■ It takes about 10 minutes.
■ Use this mixer before a meeting on materialism, money, or giving.

Here's how it works:

1. Divide into groups of four to eight people each.
2. Give each person a copy of the sheet below. It is self-explanatory.

Money Matters

Write your answers to the following statements. Then, beginning with the person who has the largest size bill ($10, $20, etc.), go clockwise around the group sharing your answers, one statement at a time.

Some images that come to mind when I hear the word "money" are . . .

When I have a lot of money, I . . .

When I don't have any money, I . . .

One thing I wish I could buy is . . .

Rich people . . .

If I won $10 million, I would . . .

God's instructions about money are . . .

Valentine's Day Extravaganza

Instructions to Leaders:

- This fun discussion mixer gives small- to medium-sized groups a chance to have fun and get better acquainted.
- It takes about 10 minutes.
- Use this mixer on or near Valentine's Day.

Here's how it works:

Give each person a copy of the sheet below. It is self-explanatory.

- -

Valentine's Day Extravaganza

Find a partner and complete the following instructions.

Get with another couple and determine which of you has had the most sweethearts.

Chat with another couple about your idea of the perfect date.

Exchange ideas with a third couple about who has the best plans for Valentine's Day.

Grab two other couples and determine which of you has the best lips.

Get with another couple and discover who has told the most people "I love you." (Note: Family members don't count!)

Meet with another couple and discuss the most romantic movie you have ever seen.

Stop a final twosome and talk about what makes a marriage work.

End-of-School Blowout

Instructions to Leaders:

■ This crazy discussion mixer gives small- to medium-sized groups a chance to have fun and get better acquainted.
■ It takes about 10 minutes.
■ Use this mixer on or near the last day of school.

Here's how it works:

Tell everyone to pair up and then give each couple a copy of the sheet below. It is self-explanatory. Note: for older groups, change the last statement to: ". . . make predictions about what you'll all be doing five years from now."

COVER THE INSTRUCTIONS ABOVE THIS LINE BEFORE PHOTOCOPYING THIS HANDOUT FOR YOUR GROUP.

- -

End-of-School Blowout

Find a partner and complete the following instructions:

Get with another couple and discuss your plans for the summer.

Stop another pair and together sing a few lines of your favorite Beach Boys song.

Have one of your twosome ride piggyback on the other and "high five" three other folks.

Grab two other couples, sit down, and quickly share (no more than 10 seconds each) "What Summer Means to Me."

Huddle with three other couples and take turns telling your most and least favorite classes of the year just concluded.

Play leapfrog with another twosome, while the four of you continue to chant, "No more pencils, no more books, no more teachers' dirty looks."

Sit down with a final pair and make predictions about where you'll all go to college and what you'll major in.

What I Did this Summer

Instructions to Leaders:

■ This discussion mixer gives small- to medium-sized groups a chance to catch up or get better acquainted.
■ It takes about 10 minutes.
■ Use this mixer on or near the first day of school.

Here's how it works:

Get your people in groups of four and have them work through the sheet below:

COVER THE INSTRUCTIONS ABOVE THIS LINE BEFORE PHOTOCOPYING THIS HANDOUT FOR YOUR GROUP.

- -

What I Did this Summer

Get into groups of four and complete the following open-ended statements:

1. The highlight of my summer was . . .
    (Begin with the person who traveled the most during June, July and August and go clockwise.)

2. The most stressful time of my summer was . . .
    (Begin with the person who has the dirtiest shoes and go counter clockwise.)

3. If I could do the summer over, I would . . .
    (Begin with the person who has the longest hair and go clockwise.)

4. My goals for the fall include . . .
    (Begin with the person who has the biggest biceps and go counter clockwise.)

Holiday Hoopla

Instructions to Leaders:

■ This discussion mixer gives small- to medium-sized groups a chance to get better acquainted.
■ It takes about 10 minutes.
■ Use this mixer just before a holiday like Easter, Labor Day, Memorial Day, New Year's Day, etc.

Here's how it works:

Arrange your people into groups of four and give the instructions verbally one at a time. Or give everyone a copy of the sheet below and have them work through it.

- -

Holiday Hoopla

Get into groups of four and work your way through the following statements:

1. Talk about what your family will do to celebrate the upcoming holiday.

2. Talk about which holiday you like best and why.

3. Talk about the holiday tradition(s) you would most like to change.

4. Talk about the most stressful aspects of various holiday celebrations.

Vacation

Instructions to Leaders:

■ This discussion-type mixer gives folks a chance to get better acquainted.
■ It takes just 10 minutes.
■ Use this mixer just before or just after those times of the year (summer, Thanksgiving, or Christmas) when families tend to travel.

Here's how it works:

Get your people in groups of four to six and have them work through the sheet below:

COVER THE INSTRUCTIONS ABOVE THIS LINE BEFORE PHOTOCOPYING THIS HANDOUT FOR YOUR GROUP.

- -

Vacation

Get into groups of four to six and work your way through the following questions:

1. If you can remember, what were the highlights and lowlights of your last family vacation?

2. Which of the following settings would be most desirable for a vacation and why: a beach area, the mountains, a big city, a resort, a cruise ship, another country?

3. What would be your ultimate dream vacation?

4. What is the worst way to travel and why?

5. What would have to happen for a family to go on vacation and actually get along, have fun together, and come back with better relationships?

Weather Weirdness

Instructions to Leaders:

■ Use this mixer to help people gain interesting insights into each other.
■ Play until someone has completed his or her sheet or until time is up.
■ Use this mixer during or just after times of strange or terrible weather.

Here's how it works:

1. Give everyone a copy of the game sheet below.
2. Inform folks to find others who can truthfully sign the statements
3. Participants may sign each sheet only once.
4. Whoever completes his or her sheet or gets the most signatures during the allotted time wins.

COVER THE INSTRUCTIONS ABOVE THIS LINE BEFORE PHOTOCOPYING THIS HANDOUT FOR YOUR GROUP.

- -

Weather Weirdness

Get autographs from individuals who possess the following secret hopes:

■ Someone who prefers rainy days:

■ Someone who has personally experienced a blizzard, hurricane, or tornado:

■ A person who has never seen snow in person:

■ Someone who likes cold weather more than hot:

■ Someone who has watched a weathercast in the last seven days:

■ A person who thinks most TV weathercasters are goofy:

■ Someone who has lived through a flood:

■ A person who is especially frightened by lightning:

■ Someone who knows what the high temperature was/will be today

■ A person who likes to look for shapes in the clouds:

■ Someone who knows what meteorology is:

Lifestyle Shopping Spree

Instructions to Leaders:

■ Use this mixer to help people gain interesting insights into each other.
■ Allow about five minutes for participants to complete their sheets and another ten for discussion.
■ Use this discussion mixer before a discussion of values or priorities.

Here's how it works:

1. Give everyone a copy of the game sheet that follows.
2. Instruct people to buy their dream lifestyle for $100.
3. Participants may only spend $100.
4. Afterward, discuss the results in groups of 6–12 using the questions at the bottom of the game sheet.

PHOTOCOPY THE REVERSE SIDE AS A HANDOUT FOR YOUR GROUP.

Lifestyle Shopping Spree

You have $100 to spend. You may "purchase" as many lifestyle items as you wish, so long as your total does not exceed $100.

Items Costing $30:

■ An annual income in the six-figure range.
■ A triathlete's body and physical fitness level.
■ A loving, attractive, and fun spouse.
■ My own business or corporation.
■ A very close relationship with God all my life.

Items Costing $20:
■ A beautiful home, professionally decorated and filled with fine furnishings.
■ Beautiful children who love and respect me and who "turn out right."
■ A Christlike impact on others (friends, family, and neighbors).
■ Three close, lifelong friends with whom I have much in common.
■ Acceptance in the right social circles and civic clubs.

Items Costing $15:
■ A long life marked by good health.
■ The chance to travel around the world.
■ Membership in a dynamic church where I am growing spiritually and helping others do the same.
■ Recognition and/or fame for some ability or accomplishment.
■ A condo (either on the beach or in the mountains).

Items Costing $5:
■ A huge walk-in closet filled with all the clothes I'd love to have.
■ My dream car.
■ A traditional family vaction every year.
■ Success in some hobby or sport.
■ A life filled with culture (fine music, great literature, and the arts).

Questions for discussion:

1. Why did you make the choices you made?
2. What makes people value different things?
3. Would it be possible to have many of the things on this sheet and still not be happy? Why or why not?
4. How attainable are the things on this sheet?
5. Could a person realistically do most or all of the things on this sheet? Why or why not?

Part Three:

LISTENING & LEARNING

Do You Know Me?

Instructions to Leaders:

■ Use this mixer in small- to medium-sized groups (8–40 people) to give people an opportunity to get to know each other on a deeper level.
■ Plan for this exercise to take more time the larger your group is.

Here's how it works:

1. Give everyone a copy of the open-ended statements below.
2. Inform participants to (a) secretly complete the sentences; (b) write their names on the handout; and (c) fold and turn in their answer sheet.
3. Have a leader read through the responses and see if the group can guess the writer of each answer sheet.

COVER THE INSTRUCTIONS ABOVE THIS LINE BEFORE PHOTOCOPYING THIS HANDOUT FOR YOUR GROUP.

- -

Do You Know Me?

Name:

1. My most valued material possession is . . .

2. The last book I read from start to finish is . . .

3. My favorite way to spend a free afternoon is . . .

4. A dream of mine is . . .

Take 5

Instructions to Leaders:

■ Use this mixer in smaller groups (8–20) to give folks an opportunity to get to know each other on a deeper level.
■ Plan for this exercise to take more time the larger your group is.

Here's how it works:

1. Give everyone a copy of the open-ended statements below.
2. Instruct participants to (a) secretly complete the sentences; (b) write their names on the handout; and (c) fold and turn in their answer sheet.
3. Have a leader read through the responses and see if the group can guess the writer of each answer sheet.

- -

Take 5

Answer any five of the following questions and then sign your name.
The group will try to guess your identity based on your responses.

Name _____

■ A secret ambition of mine is:

■ My favorite movie of all time is:

■ My dream vacation spot is:

■ My favorite food or restaurant is:

■ My hobby/hobbies is/are:

■ In ten years, I'd like to be:

■ If I had a million bucks, I'd:

■ The last book I read is:

■ A national problem I'd like to solve is:

■ My definition of commitment is:

Guess Who I Am

Instructions to Leaders:

■ Use this mixer in smaller groups (8–20 folks) to give people an opportunity to find out little-known facts about each other.

■ Plan for this exercise to take more time the larger your group is.

Here's how it works:

1. Give everyone a copy of the exercise below.
2. Have participants (a) secretly complete the sheet; (b) write their names on the handout; and (c) fold and turn in their responses.
3. Have a leader read through the responses and see if the group can guess the writer of each answer sheet.

COVER THE INSTRUCTIONS ABOVE THIS LINE BEFORE PHOTOCOPYING THIS HANDOUT FOR YOUR GROUP.

- -

Guess Who I Am

Disclose three little-known facts about yourself.
Everyone else will try to guess your identity based on your revelations.
Examples: I ran away from home when I was four or
I once was treated for rabies.

Name _____

1.

2.

3.

Favorites

Instructions to Leaders:

■ Use this mixer in smaller groups (8–20 folks) to give people an opportunity to find out some little-known facts about each other.
■ Plan for this exercise to take more time the larger your group is.

Here's how it works:

1. Give everyone a copy of the exercise below.
2. Tell participants to (a) secretly complete the sheet; (b) write their names on the handout; and (c) fold and turn in their responses.
3. Have a leader read through the responses and see if the group can guess the writer of each answer sheet.

COVER THE INSTRUCTIONS ABOVE THIS LINE BEFORE PHOTOCOPYING THIS HANDOUT FOR YOUR GROUP.

- -

Favorites

*Secretly fill in this sheet and turn it in. Everyone else will
try to guess your identity based on your responses.*

Name _____

1. My favorite singer/group is:

2. My favorite all-time movie is:

3. My favorite meal is:

4. My favorite TV show is:

5. My favorite magazine is:

6. My favorite place to visit is:

7. My favorite subject in school is/was:

Nothing but the Truth

Instructions to Leaders:

■ Use this entertaining mixer in smaller groups (8–20 members) to give folks an opportunity to find out little-known facts about each other.
■ Plan for this exercise to take more time the larger your group is.
■ This mixer is ideal for meetings dealing with honesty.

Here's how it works:

1. Give everyone a copy of the exercise below.
2. Instruct people to write four statements about themselves. Three of the statements should be true. One should be false. The group will try to determine which statement is deceptive. In other words, each individual is trying to trick the rest of the group.
3. Appoint someone to read through the responses and see if the group can guess which of the four statements is false.

COVER THE INSTRUCTIONS ABOVE THIS LINE BEFORE PHOTOCOPYING THIS HANDOUT FOR YOUR GROUP.
- -

Nothing but the Truth

Fill in this sheet with three true statements and one false.
Mix them up so that the group will have a hard time figuring out which of the four statements is the deceptive one.

Example:"I have touched a bobcat and a mountain lion" (T)
"I have been on top of the Empire State Building" (T)
"I am allergic to milk" (F)
"I would like to learn to ride a unicycle" (T)

Name _____

1.

2.

3.

4.

I Never

Instructions to Leaders:

■ Use this entertaining mixer in smaller groups (8–20 attendees) to give people an opportunity to discover little-known facts about each other.
■ Plan for this exercise to take more time the larger your group is.
■ In large groups, break up into circles of no more than 20 people each.
■ You will need 25 small objects for each player (matches, popcorn kernels, pennies, acorns, poker chips, etc.) and one big pot.

Here's how it works:

1. The object of the game is for each player to keep as many of his or her 25 small objects as possible.
2. One at a time, players will make truthful statements beginning with the phrase *"I never. . . ."* (Examples: I never have worn glasses, I never saw the movie *Ghost*, I never ate shrimp, etc.).
3. After a player makes an "I never" statement, everyone in the circle who *has* done that thing (or had that experience) must throw one of his or her kernels into a container in the middle of the circle. For instance, if a player says, "I never have snow skied," then everyone in the circle who *has been snow skiing* must throw a kernel into the pot.
4. Play at least until the first player goes out. Then see who has the most objects left.

Complete the Statement

Instructions to Leaders:

■ Use this entertaining mixer in smaller groups (8–20 members) to let people find out little-known facts about each other.

■ Plan for this exercise to take more time the larger your group is.

■ In extra large groups, break up into circles of no more than 20 people each.

Here's how it works:

1. Give everyone a copy of the exercise below.
2. Instruct everyone to (a) secretly complete the sheet; (b) write his or her name on the handout; and (c) fold and turn in his or her responses.
3. Have a person read through the responses and see if the group can guess the writer of each answer sheet.

COVER THE INSTRUCTIONS ABOVE THIS LINE BEFORE PHOTOCOPYING THIS HANDOUT FOR YOUR GROUP.

- -

Complete the Statement

Name _____

My biggest weakness:

The best advice a parent ever gave me:

The last book I read:

My hero as a kid:

The goofiest name or nickname of someone I dated:

My favorite fast food:

Complete the Statement 2

Instructions to Leaders:

■ Use this entertaining mixer in smaller groups (8–20 individuals) to help people find out little-known facts about each other.
■ Plan for this exercise to take more time the larger your group is.
■ In extra large groups, break up into circles of no more than 20 people each.

Here's how it works:

1. Give everyone a copy of the exercise below.
2. Get everyone to (a) secretly complete the sheet; (b) write his or her name on the hand-out; and (c) fold and turn in his or her responses.
3. Have a person read through the responses and see if the group can guess the writer of each answer sheet.

COVER THE INSTRUCTIONS ABOVE THIS LINE BEFORE PHOTOCOPYING THIS HANDOUT FOR YOUR GROUP.

- -

Complete the Statement 2

Name

Friends would describe me as:

The best advice I could give anyone would be:

The last movie I saw:

A zoo animal I like to watch:

A skill I wish I possessed:

My best quality is:

Past-Present-Future Game

Instructions to Leaders:

■ Use this entertaining mixer to give people an opportunity to find out little-known facts about each other's past, present, or future.
■ Break up into groups of 4–6 people to best utilize this mixer.
■ Play for a set time limit—10 or 15 minutes.

Here's how it works:

Provide a set of the "questions" below (cut-out and separated by category) for each small group.

COVER THE INSTRUCTIONS ABOVE THIS LINE BEFORE PHOTOCOPYING THIS HANDOUT FOR YOUR GROUP.

- -

Past-Present-Future Game

Instructions:

1. Take turns answering questions, beginning with the youngest person in each group. He or she can choose from any of the three categories.
2. That person then chooses a category (and question) for the person to his or her left to answer.
3. Continue in a like manner until your leader calls time.

Questions about the past:
What is your earliest memory?
What were you like as a baby?
What is the happiest time you can remember?
When were you the saddest?
What is something you regret?
What is your greatest achievement?
Who was your favorite teacher in elementary school and why?
When did you first start thinking seriously about God?
What did you believe about Santa Claus as a child?
If you believed in Santa, how did you feel when you found out he is make believe?
What were your feelings about church as a child?
What were you like as a child from the ages of 8–10?
What was your favorite game as a little kid?
What were some of the things you said you were going to be when you grew up?
What is the lowest price you can remember (in your lifetime) for a gallon of gas? For a canned soft drink? For a candy bar?

Questions about the present:
What is something you enjoy doing?
What relationship means a lot to you and why?
How would you rate your spiritual life right now? Why?
What is your favorite kind of music?
How much TV do you watch per week? What kinds of programs?
What is something that really makes you mad?
What part of the newspaper do you read first?
What do you do with the money that comes your way?
What world problem do you worry about most?
What is the biggest problem facing your friends?
What quality or characteristic about yourself are you satisfied with?
What is a typical Friday night like for you?
Rank these items according to your current priorities: school; work; friends; family; God; church; extracurricular activities; romance.
What hassles are in your life right now?
How much do you spend on entertainment in an average week?

Questions about the future:
What scares you about the future?
What excites you about the future?
Where would you like to settle down?
What career do you dream about?
When will you marry?
What will you do after graduation?
What skills would you like to learn?
What will you be like in 10 years?
What is one thing you want to do before you die?
How many kids will you have?
How long do you think you will live?
What is a goal you have for the next year?
What kind of world do you think your children will inherit?
If given the chance for space travel, would you do it? Why or why not?
What (realistically) do you think you will earn per year when you are at the summit of your career?

EMOTIONS!

Instructions to Leaders:

■ Use this informative mixer to give folks an opportunity to find out little-known facts about each other's feelings.
■ Break up into groups of four to best utilize this mixer.
■ Play for a set time limit, say, 7–10 minutes.

Here's how it works:

Provide a copy of the sheet below to each person

COVER THE INSTRUCTIONS ABOVE THIS LINE BEFORE PHOTOCOPYING THIS HANDOUT FOR YOUR GROUP.

- -

EMOTIONS!

Form a foursome and complete these open-ended statements on your sheet.
Then have each person share at least three "emotions" with the group.

Something that really makes me **nervous** is:

I get **depressed** when:

What really **ticks me off** is:

The times I feel **happiest** are when:

I'm **bored** whenever:

To me, the most **frustrating** thing is:

What Would You Do?

Instructions to Leaders:

■ Use this informative mixer to give people an opportunity to find out little-known facts about each other.
■ Break up into groups of 4–6 to best utilize this mixer.
■ Play for a set time limit, say, 7–10 minutes.

Here's how it works:

Provide one copy of the sheet below to each group.

COVER THE INSTRUCTIONS ABOVE THIS LINE BEFORE PHOTOCOPYING THIS HANDOUT FOR YOUR GROUP.

- -

What Would You Do?

Instructions:

■ The person in your group who has the smallest feet goes first.
■ He or she must answer the first question below.
■ He or she must then give this question sheet to someone else in the group.
■ That person must then answer question #2.
■ Continue in this manner until everyone has responded to at least one hypothetical situation.

1. (For men) What would you do if you asked out someone special for a first date and after eating a nice meal in a fancy restaurant, you realized you didn't have your wallet? (For women) What would you do if you were driving alone on the interstate all by yourself at night and your car broke down five miles from the nearest phone?
2. What would you do if a date of yours got sloppy drunk and started doing some really embarrassing things in front of a bunch of your friends?
3. What would you do if you dropped a tray of food in front of 350 other people?
4. What would you do if you saw an engaged friend of yours deep kissing someone other than his or her fiancée or fiancé?
5. What would you do if you won $10,000,000 in a sweepstakes?
6. What would you do (honestly) if someone offered you $1,000 to ride naked on a motorcycle (no helmet!) across town during rush hour? What if the person offered you *$10,000?*
7. What would you do if you lost, broke, wrecked, or destroyed your most precious material possession? (First, name what that possession is.)
8. What would you do if someone falsely accused you of a horrible crime?
9. What would you do if Jay Leno asked you to come on *The Tonight Show* as a guest?
10. What would you do if you were trapped on Gilligan's Island with Gilligan, the Skipper, and the other castaways?

Scenarios

Instructions to Leaders:

■ Use this informative mixer to give people an opportunity to find out little-known facts about each other.
■ Break up into groups of 4-8 to best utilize this mixer.
■ Play for a set time limit, say, 7-10 minutes.

Here's how it works:

Provide one copy of the sheet below to each group.

- -

Scenarios

In groups of 4-8, take eight minutes to answer the following questions. Begin with the person who has been to Disney World and/or Disneyland the most number of times. Proceed clockwise until time runs out, or until you have answered all of the questions.

1. What would you do if . . . you were in a convenience store and a masked gunman suddenly came in to rob the place?
2. What would you do if . . . someone broke a date with you to go out with a friend of yours?
3. What would you do if . . . your car broke down in the worst part of town at night?
4. What would you do if . . . your house or apartment burned down and everything you owned was gone?
5. What would you do if . . . our entire economy collapsed and we found ourselves in the middle of a Great Depression?
6. What would you do if . . . you wrecked a friend's car which you weren't supposed to be driving?
7. What would you do if . . . you found a wallet with no I.D. and $200 in it?
8. What would you do if . . . your family suddenly had to move 1,000 miles away?
9. What would you do if . . . a war broke out and you were drafted?
10. What would you do if . . . you were given an opportunity to address the leaders of the ten most powerful countries in the world?
11. What would you do if . . . a close friend announced he/she has AIDS?
12. What would you do if . . . a wealthy individual told you he/she would pay for you to go to any educational institution in the world and study whatever you wanted?

Extremities

Instructions to Leaders:

■ Use this eye-opening discussion mixer to get people talking about their personality types.
■ Keep each discussion group small—no more than 10–12 per group.

Here's how it works:

1. Break your big group into small groups (10–12 people each).
2. Give everyone a copy of the exercise below.
3. After they circle the appropriate words, have participants take turns sharing their responses.

COVER THE INSTRUCTIONS ABOVE THIS LINE BEFORE PHOTOCOPYING THIS HANDOUT FOR YOUR GROUP.

- -

Extremities

In each pair of words (for example, CBS and PBS), circle the one which you are most like. (Note: The idea here is not to choose a favorite, but to select the one that better fits your personality, personal tastes, or lifestyle.)

CBS	PBS
Steak-N-Ale	Burger King
Ghost	Terminator 2
Democrat	Republican
Peanuts	The Far Side
Wal-Mart	Saks Fifth Avenue
Rolex	Timex
King James Version	The Living Bible
Non-fat yogurt	Ice cream
French poodle	Labrador Retriever
The symphony	A tractor pull
Mountains	Beach
City	Country
Formal wear	Blue jeans
Beethoven	Garth Brooks
Stand-up comic	Accountant
Stamp collector	Bungee jumper
Rocker/recliner	Folding chair
Winter	Summer
Interstate Highway	Gravel road
Cellular Phone	Handwritten letter
The mall	The library
Michael Jackson	Fred Astaire
Vegetable garden	Flower garden
Scrabble	Boxing

Fears!

Instructions to Leaders:
- ■ Use this eye-opening discussion mixer to get people talking about what scares them.
- ■ Keep the discussion groups small—4–8 people each.
- ■ This mixer works well around Halloween or before any discussion having to do with fear.

Here's how it works:
1. Break your big group into small groups (4-8 people each).
2. Give everyone a copy of the exercise below.
3. Instruct participants to take turns sharing their responses.
4. Discuss the questions that follow in the small groups.

COVER THE INSTRUCTIONS ABOVE THIS LINE BEFORE PHOTOCOPYING THIS HANDOUT FOR YOUR GROUP.

- -

 # *Fears!*

Complete the following chart by checking how afraid you are of each item listed.
1 represents "not scared a bit"; 10 means "terrified—shaking in my boots!"

Item	1	2	3	4	5	6	7	8	9	10
Failure (in general)										
Not having/losing friends										
Not doing well in school										
Economic hard times										
Going to war										
Death (either my own or someone close to me)										
Getting cancer/AIDS or some other disease										
Not fitting in										
Parents divorcing										
Public speaking										
Other (specify):										

Have participants discuss (voluntarily) this mixer in their small groups using the following questions:
1. According to this chart, what things are you not worried about at all? Why?
2. According to this chart, what things really trouble you? Why?
3. What's the difference between being "concerned" and being "terrified"?
4. Why do we fear different things?
5. How can your confidence in one area help someone who is struggling in that area?
6. What is the best advice you could give to someone overcome by fear?

OPINIONS!

Instructions to Leaders:

■ Use this informative mixer to give folks an opportunity to find out about each other's opinions.
■ Break up into groups of four to best utilize this mixer.
■ Play for a set time limit, say, 10-12 minutes.

Here's how it works:

Provide a copy of the sheet below to each person

COVER THE INSTRUCTIONS ABOVE THIS LINE BEFORE PHOTOCOPYING THIS HANDOUT FOR YOUR GROUP.

OPINIONS!

Form a foursome and take 20–30 seconds apiece summarizing your opinions concerning each of the following institutions.

1. School

2. Government

3. Hollywood

4. Madison Avenue (the advertising industry)

5. The Church

Agree-Disagree

Instructions to Leaders:

- Use this interesting mixer to let people see where they and their peers stand on certain "hot" issues.
- You can play this game with a big group (and have them raise hands, stand up, or move to one side of the room or the other), but peer pressure can sometimes prevent people from answering honestly. To encourage honesty you may wish to have your group sit in a circle, write their answers on scratch paper, and hold all the answers up at the same time.
- Play until you have worked through all the statements below.
- This exercise prompts plenty of debate and lends itself to natural follow-up questions (for example, "Those of you who said, 'Agree,' why do you feel that way?" etc.)
- For extra effect, use this prior to a meeting on conflict!

COVER THE INSTRUCTIONS ABOVE THIS LINE BEFORE PHOTOCOPYING THIS HANDOUT FOR YOUR GROUP.

- -

Agree-Disagree

1. Spanking should definitely be used to discipline kids.

2. Public schools should begin each day with a time of silence (for prayer or meditation).

3. Since kids are going to have sex anyway, they should be given condoms and encouraged to use them.

4. If the choice is between saving a few hundred jobs or saving an endangered species, we should choose to save the endangered species.

5. If people don't like what they see on TV, they should just turn it off.

6. The millions of dollars we spend each year in this country to feed and pamper *pets* could better be used to help homeless, starving people.

7. Despite the First Amendment, soft porn magazines like *Playboy* and *Penthouse* should be banned.

8. Violence on TV or in movies contributes to a more violent society.

9. Couples should divorce if they are incompatible.

10. Schools should promote moral values.

Affirmation

Instructions to Leaders:

■ Use this enjoyable mixer to both encourage people in your group and teach the art of encouragement!

■ This exercise works best with smaller groups (8–25 people) who know each other fairly well.

■ For extra effect, use this mixer prior to a meeting on encouragement or loving each other!

Here's how it works:

1. Tape to the walls around the room pieces of poster board, newsprint, or butcher paper.

2. Down the side of each sheet write the name of someone at the meeting.

3. Give everyone a pen or marker and tell them to write on each person's sheet an encouraging word that begins with one or two of the letters in that person's name.

4. When completed the sheets will look like this:

Bold, best friend	**K**ind
Real, remembers others	**A**lways smiling
Assertive	**R**isk-taker, righteous
Diligent, does good to others	**I**ntelligent, interesting
	Not worried about what others think, nice

People Power!

Instructions to Leaders:

■ Use this enjoyable mixer to both encourage people in your group and teach the art of encouragement!

■ This exercise works best with smaller groups (8–25 people) who know each other fairly well.

■ For extra effect, use this prior to a meeting on encouragement or loving each other!

Here's how it works:

1. Sit in a circle.
2. Distribute sheets of paper. Have everyone write their names at the top of their papers.
3. Begin passing the sheets around the circle (left or right, it doesn't matter so long as everyone is going the same direction).
4. Under the name on the top of the sheet, have people write truthful (but positive) comments about that person.
5. When the sheets get back around to their owners, have each individual read off what has been written about him or her. This is difficult for most people. Some will become quite embarrassed. But this is a great exercise in learning to accept affirmation, and people always feel great when they leave a meeting where this has been done.
6. Completed sheets will look like this:

Shawna Burch

Funny, fun to be around

Sensitive

Caring, concerned for others

Great sense of humor

Beautiful smile

Mischievous

A natural leader

Growing as a Christian

Kind, compassionate

Always makes me smile

Faithful

The Chair of Encouragement

Instructions to Leaders:

■ Use this enjoyable mixer to both encourage people in your group and teach the art of encouragement!

■ This exercise works best with smaller groups (8–25 folks) who know each other fairly well.

■ For best results, use this at the end of a retreat or a time of ministry together.

Here's how it works:

1. Sit in a circle.
2. Put one person in the middle of the circle in a chair.
3. Go around the circle and have each person share one thing they appreciate about the person in the "chair of encouragement."
4. This is difficult for most people. Some will become quite embarrassed being the center of attention. But this is a great exercise in learning to accept affirmation, and people always feel great when they leave a meeting where this has been done.
5. You may wish to have a box of tissues on hand. This exercise can be very emotional!

Question Tag

Instructions to Leaders:

■ Use this fast-paced, unpredictable mixer to help the people in your group get to know each other on a deeper level.

■ This exercise works best with smaller groups numbering 10–20.

Here's how it works:

1. Sit in a circle (or circles if you need to break down into several small groups).
2. Give each group a copy of the handout on the following page.

Question Tag

*Directions: When you are asked a question, you **must** answer. You then have the opportunity to ask anyone else in the group any question on this page—including the same question you have just answered.*

- What was your favorite pet and why?
- What would be your ideal, ultimate job?
- How many kids would you like to have?
- How would you best like to spend a free afternoon?
- Where would you like to honeymoon?
- What is your favorite magazine?
- What is your favorite sport and why?
- What things scare you and why?
- In your opinion, what ingredients make a romantic relationship work?
- What would be your least preferred way of dying?
- What kind of dogs do you like most and least and why?
- Would you prefer money, fame, or power and why?
- How important is money to you?
- If you could have either three terrific, loyal, lifelong friends or $1 million, which would you pick and why?
- Have you ever shoplifted? What?
- Have you ever skinny-dipped? Where and when?
- How would you improve your school?
- How would you improve life in this city?
- If you had to give up one of your senses, which would you part with and why?
- If you could become world-famous in one of these fields (sports, medicine, politics, business, finance, entertainment, law, cooking, or military), which would you pick and why?
- What is the best advice you ever got?
- Why do so few people seem interested in God and/or spiritual matters?
- What makes for a happy home?
- What is the most exciting experience you have ever had?
- Would you consider moving to a third world country? Why or why not?
- What is your typical bedtime routine?
- What is your typical morning routine?
- What one question would you like to ask God?
- What one word pops into your mind when you hear the phrase "the Bible"?
- How would you go about reducing racial tension in this country?
- Should drugs be legalized? Why or why not?
- Where is the most beautiful place you have ever visited?
- In what state would you like to live?
- What could churches do to attract more young people?
- What is your favorite season and why?

Question Throw

Instructions to Leaders:

■ Use this fast-paced, unpredictable mixer to help the people in your group get to know each other on a deeper level.

■ This exercise works best with smaller groups (8–12 each).

■ Play for 10 to 12 minutes.

Here's how it works:

1. Have your group sit in a circle (or circles if you need to break down into several smaller groups).
2. Give each group a paper cup full of the questions below. (Copy and cut so that questions are separated.)
3. Give each group a ball (tennis, ping-pong, racquetball, etc.).
4. Explain that one person from each group should volunteer to go first. He or she will draw a question from the cup and answer it. Then that individual will toss the ball to someone else (anyone) within the group. The new "questionee" has a choice: answer a spontaneous question from the person who threw him or her the ball or answer a prepared question which the thrower will draw from the cup.

COVER THE INSTRUCTIONS ABOVE THIS LINE BEFORE PHOTOCOPYING THIS HANDOUT FOR YOUR GROUP.

- -

Question Throw

■ At what age do you think you will marry and why?

■ What would be your idea of the perfect meal?

■ What person would you like to swap places with for one day?

■ Describe the happiest day in your life.

■ If you could spend a week during any period in history, what era would you choose and why?

■ What are three foods you absolutely cannot stand?

■ Who, in your opinion, is the greatest leader in the world today? Why?

■ Describe what the perfect day would be like for you?

■ Predict what your life will be like 20 years from now.

■ What three things really irritate you?

■ What is the best family vacation you ever took and why?

■ What three things would you absolutely not do for a million bucks?

■ What, in your opinion, are the worst ways to die?

■ What is the worst smell you have ever encountered?

■ What food/meal/dessert are you most skilled at making?

■ If your best friend were unjustly jailed, what would you do?

■ How would you respond if someone here started choking?

■ What is the secret to a happy family? Why?

■ What kinds of things make your day?

Who?

Instructions to Leaders:

■ Use this mixer to help the people in your group get to know each other on a deeper level.
■ This exercise works best with smaller groups (4–8 people each).

Here's how it works:

1. Sit in a circle (or circles if you need to break down into several small groups).
2. Give each group one copy of the sheet below.

COVER THE INSTRUCTIONS ABOVE THIS LINE BEFORE PHOTOCOPYING THIS HANDOUT FOR YOUR GROUP.

- -

Who?

In your small group, take 7–10 minutes to answer the following questions.
The person in your group who is oldest should answer number one.
The person to his or her left will then answer the second question.
Continue until everyone has responded to at least one question.

1. Who (if you could pick any living person) would you like to see leading this country?

2. Who, in your opinion, is the greatest living actor/actress?

3. Who has had the greatest influence on you?

4. Who would you like to trade places with for one day?

5. (For a female) Who is the handsomest man in the world?
   (For a male) Who is the most beautiful woman in the world?

6. Who is somebody famous who gets on your nerves?

7. Who is someone who always makes you feel better?

8. Who do you turn to when your world is crumbling?

9. Who is the best teacher you ever had and why?

10. Who is the most spiritual person you know?

11. Who, in your opinion, has the greatest smile?

12. Who has a lifestyle that you'd like to emulate?

What?

Instructions to Leaders:

■ Use this mixer to help the people in your group get to know each other on a deeper level.

■ This exercise works best with smaller groups (4-8 people each).

Here's how it works:

1. Sit in a circle (or circles if you need to break down into several small groups).
2. Give each group a copy of the sheet below.

COVER THE INSTRUCTIONS ABOVE THIS LINE BEFORE PHOTOCOPYING THIS HANDOUT FOR YOUR GROUP.

- -

What?

In your small group (after introducing yourselves to each other), take 7–10 minutes to answer the following questions. The person who has the nearest upcoming birthday gets to go first. Then proceed with the next person (clockwise) and the second question. Continue until everyone has answered at least one question.

1. What was your first impression of the people in this room?

2. What could be done (if anything) to stop the crime problem in this country?

3. What, in your opinion, is the biggest reason people don't make God a priority in their lives?

4. What do you know about your ancestral heritage?

5. What kind of pets would you like to have (and absolutely *not* have)?

6. What do you think you will miss most about this place when you eventually leave?

7. What foods will you positively refuse to eat?

8. What are you best and worst at?

9. What three new stores, restaurants, etc. would you like to have in town?

10. What factors make a party a "really good" party?

11. What magazines do you like to read on a regular basis?

12. What trips/vacations are you planning to take in the next year?

When?

Instructions to Leaders:

■ Use these "when?" questions to help the people in your group get to know each other on a deeper level.
■ This exercise works best with smaller groups (4-8 people each).

Here's how it works:

1. Sit in a circle (or circles if you need to break down into several small groups).
2. Give each group a copy of the sheet below.

- -

When?

*In small groups of 4–8, take a few minutes to answer the following questions.
Begin with the person who is the youngest. Proceed counter-clockwise
until time runs out, or until you have answered all of the questions.*

1. When do you think the most and why? (For example, when driving, just before bed, etc.)

2. When are you the most peaceful?

3. When do you get really angry?

4. When do you think a romantic relationship should be broken off?

5. When is it appropriate to confront someone about his or her wrong behavior?

6. When is it most difficult for you to make a decision?

7. When is it right for a couple to become physically involved in their relationship?

8. When do you plan to decide on a career?

9. When (if ever) do you think war is necessary?

10. When should kids learn the facts of life (and sex)?

11. When is the best time to talk to someone about spiritual matters?

12. When are you the happiest?

Where?

Instructions to Leaders:

■ Use these "where?" questions to help the people in your group get to know each other on a deeper level.
■ This exercise works best with smaller groups (4–8 people each).

Here's how it works:

1. Sit in a circle (or circles if you need to break down into several small groups).
2. Give each group a copy of the sheet below.

COVER THE INSTRUCTIONS ABOVE THIS LINE BEFORE PHOTOCOPYING THIS HANDOUT FOR YOUR GROUP.

- -

Where?

In small groups of 4–8, take eight minutes to answer the following questions.
Begin with the person who has most recently flown on an airplane.
Proceed counter-clockwise until time runs out, or
until you have answered all of the questions.

1. Where is the most peaceful place you have been?

2. Where do you like to go when you want to have fun?

3. Where do you like to go when you want to sort things out?

4. Where should our government leaders be spending most of their time and attention?

5. Where did your happiest memories occur?

6. Where does one find the ideal boyfriend/girlfriend?

7. Where is the ideal honeymoon spot?

8. Where (in your opinion) is the most beautiful scenery on earth?

9. Where would you turn if you were extremely confused or depressed?

10. Where would you like to be ten years from today?

11. Where do you and your friends hang out most often?

12. Where would you go if you won a free trip to anywhere?

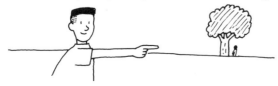

Why?

Instructions to Leaders:

■ Use this mixer to help the people in your group get to know each other on a deeper level.
■ This exercise works best with smaller groups (4–8 people each).

Here's how it works:

1. Sit in a circle (or circles if you need to break down into several small groups).
2. Give each group a copy of the sheet below.

- -

Why?

In your small group, take 7–10 minutes to answer the following questions. The person who lives the farthest away from where you are now sitting should answer number one. The person to his or her left answers number two. Continue until everyone has answered a question.

1. Why do you think professional wrestling is so popular in this country?

2. Why do you think so many people report having seen UFOs?

3. Why do the U.S. Supreme Court and Congress begin each day with prayer, and yet public schools are not allowed to begin with prayer?

4. Why do you think so many people are turned off by church?

5. Why do most people get so upset when discussing the abortion issue?

6. Why do girls go to the restroom in mass numbers?

7. Why, in your opinion, does Michael Jackson choose to look and act so strange?

8. Why would you (or would you not) want to become President of the United States?

9. Why are there so many divorces?

10. Why do some people cry in movies while others don't?

11. Why do some guys find it so difficult to make commitments?

12. Why are some people so opposed to God?

How?

Instructions to Leaders:

■ Use this mixer to help the people in your group get to know each other on a deeper level.
■ This exercise works best with smaller groups (4–8 people each).

Here's how it works:

1. Sit in a circle (or circles if you need to break down into several small groups).
2. Give each group a copy of the sheet below.

COVER THE INSTRUCTIONS ABOVE THIS LINE BEFORE PHOTOCOPYING THIS HANDOUT FOR YOUR GROUP.

– –

How?

In your small group (after introducing yourselves to each other), take 7–10 minutes to answer the following questions. The person wearing the brightest colors goes first. Then proceed with the next person (counter-clockwise) and the second question. Continue until everyone has answered at least one question.

1. How should disobedient children be disciplined?

2. How (specifically) would you respond to a date offer you did not wish to accept?

3. How could the education system in this country be improved?

4. How do you pick your friends?

5. How much homework should schools give?

6. How much prejudice and racism do you see in everyday life?

7. How likely is it that you will ever feel financially secure?

8. How will you decide what to do after you finish here?

9. How do (did) you decide whom to date?

10. How come most females can't stand the Three Stooges and most males like them?

11. How hard is it for you to save money?

12. How much sleep do you require to stay reasonably sane?

If?

Instructions to Leaders:

■ Use these "if" questions to help your group relate on a deeper level.
■ This exercise works best with smaller groups (4–8 people each).

Here's how it works:

1. Sit in a circle (or circles if you need to break down into several small groups).
2. Give each group a copy of the sheet below.

COVER THE INSTRUCTIONS ABOVE THIS LINE BEFORE PHOTOCOPYING THIS HANDOUT FOR YOUR GROUP.

- -

If?

*In your small group, introduce yourselves and then answer the following
"if" questions. The person with the most money on him/her goes first.
Proceed clockwise with the next person and question until everyone
in the group has answered at least one question.*

1. If you found you had one week left to live, how would you spend your final days?

2. If you saw someone shoplifting, how would you respond?

3. If you could ask God one question (and get an answer), what would it be?

4. If you were stranded on a desert island with any three possessions, what would you want?

5. If you were locked in a high-rise elevator for the weekend with two other people, who would you prefer to be stuck with and why?

6. If you could live at any time in history, what period would you choose and why?

7. If you could rewrite history in some way, what event would you want to change and why?

8. If you had thirty seconds of free air time on all three networks during prime time, what would you want to say?

9. If you had to give up one of your senses, which would you part with and why?

10. If you could cure any one disease, which would you eliminate and why?

11. If you could attend any great sporting event, which would you choose and why?

12. If your sweetheart was horribly disfigured in an accident, how do you think you would handle it? (*Would* you be able to?)

Tell Me This

Instructions to Leaders:

■ Use this mixer to give the people in your group a chance to ask each other questions and find out little-known facts about each other.
■ This exercise works best with groups ranging from 12–25 individuals.
■ This exercise can go on for as long as you like.

Here's how it works:

1. Sit in a circle (or circles if you need to break down into several small groups).

2. Give each person a sheet of paper and have everyone write his or her name at the top.

3. Then give the group an instruction like "Pass your sheet four people to the right" or "Pass your sheet three people to the left."

4. When the papers have been passed, have everyone write a question to the person whose sheet they are now holding (the name will be at the top).

5. After doing this three or four times, return the sheets to their owners and go around the circle having each person answer the questions on their sheet.

APPENDICES

Appendix 1:

Tips for Dividing into Smaller Groups

A few of the mixers in this book are most effective when used in groups of four to twelve people. Because of this fact, you will often want to divide your big group into several smaller groups. This can be done a number of ways (see below), but always remember these three guidelines:

1. Make sure that you don't end up with a group composed entirely of introverts. If necessary, assign one or two outgoing individuals to each small group to guarantee that the conversation flows.

2. Encourage people to break out of their comfort zones and get to know someone new. Cliquish behavior is normal and often leads to deep friendships, but it also inhibits the formation of *new* relationships. Try—as much as possible—to give people the security of knowing one or two folks in their small group, but also stretch them a bit by teaming them up with one or two individuals they don't know well.

3. Have a definite plan for breaking up into small groups *before your meeting begins*. Otherwise you will lose a lot of time trying to herd everyone into the right place.

Dividing into Two Groups:
- Count off (1, 2 . . . 1, 2)
- Males/Females
- Brown-eyed people/everybody else
- Last name A–L/Last name M–Z
- Those with a driver's license/those without
- Upperclassmen/Freshmen
- Seniors/Everyone else
- Cat lovers/dog lovers
- Number everyone—odd numbers in one group, even numbers in another

Dividing into Four Groups:
- Count off (1, 2, 3, 4 . . . 1, 2, 3, 4).
- By year in school (9th, 10th, 11th, 12th)
- Hair color (black, brown, blonde, red)
- Colored dots (four colors)
- Soft drink preference (Coke, Pepsi, 7-Up, Dr. Pepper)

Dividing into Six Groups:
- Count off (1, 2, 3, 4, 5, 6 . . . 1, 2, 3, 4, 5, 6).
- Play "Barnyard at Night" (using six animal sounds)—see page 25.
- By birth month (Jan/Feb; March/April; May/June; etc.)
- Colored dots (six different colors)
- By college (for university students—College of Arts & Sciences, College of Business, etc.)

Appendix 2:

101 Questions & Discussion Starters

1. What is your favorite dessert and why?
2. What is your favorite holiday and why?
3. If you could be anywhere else in the world right now, where would you want to be and why?
4. What is one thing that really ticks you off?
5. What is your favorite athletic activity?
6. What impulsive thing have you done this week?
7. Describe the time in your life when you were the coldest.
8. What was your best Christmas ever and why?
9. What would you do if you were President for a day?
10. Look back and describe yourself in the third grade.
11. What are your three best qualities?
12. Finish this statement: People probably think I _____.
13. The most daring thing I ever did was _____.
14. If I could give anyone anything, I would give _____ to _____.
15. The time I felt closest to God was when:
16. I worry most about:
17. Three adjectives I would use to describe myself are:
18. I think heaven will be:
19. If I could own any type of business, it would be:
20. Summer is great because:
21. I last cried because:
22. What quality from your parents' marriage would you not want to repeat in your own marriage?
23. What quality from your parents' marriage would you want to repeat in your own marriage?
24. I am most relaxed when:
25. The easiest subject at school is:
26. Something I'll never understand is:
27. What excites you? Why?
28. What Bible book do you like most?
29. What Bible character would you like to have lunch with and why?
30. Are you more like your mom or dad? Why do you say that?
31. What bad habit would you like to change about yourself?
32. When did you feel the proudest?
33. What do you admire most about your parents?
34. What annual income would satisfy you? Why?
35. What qualities make for a great friendship?
36. Why are premarital sex and adultery so common?
37. Who is your most respected spiritual leader?
38. How (if at all) can a couple "divorce-proof" their marriage?

39. Do you think you'll divorce? Why or why not?
40. The best pet is:
41. The best restaurant is:
42. I get sad when:
43. Who makes you laugh the most?
44. The person whose life I have most influenced is _____.Why?
45. TV could be improved if:
46. What is your favorite beverage? Why?
47. How much influence do your friends have on you? Why?
48. My parents would describe me as:
49. A weakness I have is:
50. What is the best month of the year? Why?
51. What is your most vivid memory of childhood?
52. What is your favorite flower?
53. When were you most embarrassed and why?
54. What do you like most and least about this group?
55. Who would you want for a bodyguard if you had to walk through New York city on foot?
56. What makes a leader?
57. What is the formula for romantic success?
58. A person I admire is:
59. I stress out whenever:
60. I laugh whenever I remember:
61. I think I will live until the age of:
62. A food that makes me gag is:
63. What is your biggest struggle right now?
64. What are you proudest of?
65. What are you like when you first wake up?
66. What is your opinion of country music?
67. Why are so many murders committed annually in this country?
68. How would you explain the Holy Spirit?
69. Why do you believe in God?
70. What would Jesus say to us right now if he were physically present?
71. When do you think the world will end and why?
72. What is the most disappointed you have ever been?
73. How much cheating goes on in your school?
74. What is the best show on television?
75. Who is the most talented person you know?
76. What in your life needs to change?
77. I get angry when:
78. *Peace* means:
79. I would define *joy* as:
80. Something I don't deserve is:
81. What would you like to change about your physical appearance?
82. Why do you or do you not feel you can be honest with this group?
83. I hate:

84. What is the best book you ever read and why?
85. What I like and don't like about my hair is:
86. The closest thing to a miracle I've ever seen was when:
87. What is your favorite color?
88. What are your views on the death penalty?
89. When, if ever, is war justified?
90. What do you think about the animal rights movement?
91. What are your views on gun control?
92. How would you try to eliminate racism?
93. What do you think hell is like?
94. What is love?
95. What is the best approach to stopping AIDS?
96. What makes a good group?
97. What do you do to occupy time when you are driving?
98. What is one of your most recent daydreams?
99. What is something you wish you could do?
100. How much marital infidelity really goes on and why?
101. Grandparents are: